# Ism you or Ism me

## Overcoming Our Hatred For Each Other's Economic Ideals and Synthesizing an Economy For the Future

by Dr. Jeremy Dean Harrison

EST 2024

CHOZEH ROEH

BOOK PUBLISHING · IP MANAGEMENT

Ism you or Ism me
Overcoming Our Hatred For Each Other's Economic Ideals and Synthesizing an Economy For the Future

Published by Chozeh Roeh



Published in the United States by Chozeh Roeh, Southern Utah.
Printed in the United States of America.



Library of Congress Cataloging in Publication Data
Harrison, Jeremy Dean.
Ism you or Ism me
Overcoming Our Hatred For Each Other's Economic Ideals and Synthesizing an Economy For the Future

ISBN: 978-1-966904-00-7

Dedicated to my wife and children, who have given me the inspiration to create this book. Without your love and support, it would not be worth it. Let us learn from our dreams, ambitions, and history to make a better world for the future.

**Table of Contents**

Introduction....................................................................9
- The Quest for Utopia: An Overview
- The Historical Context of Economic Ideologies
- Philosophical Foundations and Misinterpretations

Chapter 1: The Philosophical Underpinnings of Economic Systems...........................................25
- Historical Context and Misinterpretations
- Common Ground and Divergence
- Toward a Utopian Vision: Synthesis of Ideals
- Overcoming Human Interference
- The Convergence of Ideals

Chapter 2: Historical Case Studies..........................................54
- The Soviet Experiment: Successes and Failures
- The Rise of Capitalism: Industrial Revolution to Present
- Socialism in Scandinavia: A Hybrid Model
- Lessons Learned from Historical Implementations

Chapter 3: The Role of Technology in Shaping Economic Systems..................................61
- The Impact of Industrialization and Automation
- The Digital Revolution: Blockchain and Beyond
- Technology and Transparency: Ensuring Fair Contributions
- Future Prospects: AI and the Economy

Chapter 4: Economic Theories and Models............................67
- Classical and Neoclassical Economics
- Marxist Economic Theory
- Contemporary Economic Thought
- Integrating Economic Theories for a New Model

Chapter 5: The Concept of a Contribution-Based System.........72
- Defining Contribution-Based Economics
- Mechanisms for Measuring Contributions
- Digital Contracts and Blockchain: Ensuring Fairness

- Case Studies: Successful Implementation of Contribution Models

Chapter 6: Overcoming Human Interference........................82
- The Role of Governance and Regulation
- Mitigating Corruption and Greed
- Promoting Ethical Practices in Economics
- Creating Systems Resistant to Exploitation

Chapter 7: Synthesizing Communism and Capitalism..............87
- The Ideals of Communism and Capitalism
- Harmonizing Collective and Individual Interests
- Practical Steps Toward Synthesis
- Vision of a Converged Economic System

Chapter 8: The Path to Utopia..........................................93
- Theoretical Foundations of Utopian Societies
- Practical Challenges and Solutions
- The Role of Global Cooperation and Community
- Final Reflections: Is Utopia Achievable?

Conclusion.........................................................103
- Summary of Key Insights
- The Future of Economic Systems
- Call to Action: Building a Fair and Equitable Society

Appendices.........................................................108
- Appendix A: Glossary of Terms
- Appendix B: Detailed Case Studies
- Appendix C: Methodology for Measuring Contributions
- Appendix D: Additional Resources and Readings

## Introduction

## The Quest for Utopia

The pursuit of a perfect society, Zion, or utopia has been a driving force behind human civilization's intellectual and practical endeavors. This quest has inspired a plethora of economic ideologies, each proposing a unique vision for achieving societal well-being and justice. The term Utopia was first coined by Sir Thomas More in his book Utopia, which described an imaginary island with a perfect socio-political and legal system. Sir Thomas More's Utopia, first published in 1516, presents a dynamic vision of an ideal society set on the imaginary island.
Utopia has been the subject of extensive scholarly analysis, as it offers profound insights into More's critique of contemporary European society and his aspirations for a better world.

Sir Thomas More (1478-1535) was an English lawyer, philosopher, statesman, and humanist. Utopia was written during the Renaissance, a period marked by a flourishing of arts, culture, and intellectual inquiry. This era saw the rise of humanism, which emphasized the value of human beings and the pursuit of knowledge. More's involvement in the humanist movement significantly influenced his writing of Utopia.

Utopia is structured as a dialogue between More and a traveler named Raphael Hythloday, who describes the island of Utopia and its society. The name Utopia, derived from Greek, means no place or nowhere, indicating that the island is an idealized, fictional construct. This dialogue format allows More to juxtapose the ideal society of Utopia with the flawed realities of 16th- century Europe.

The Renaissance and Humanism

The Renaissance was a period of remarkable cultural and intellectual growth in Europe, characterized by a renewed interest in the classical knowledge of ancient Greece and Rome. This revival, known as humanism, placed a strong emphasis on the study of humanities— literature, history, philosophy, and art.

Humanists believed in the potential for human beings to achieve greatness through education, ethical living, and civic engagement.

Prominent figures of the Renaissance, such as Erasmus, Leonardo da Vinci, and Michelangelo, exemplified the humanist spirit. They sought to harmonize classical wisdom with contemporary thought, fostering a culture that celebrated human creativity and intellect. Humanism encouraged a critical examination of traditional beliefs and institutions, promoting the idea that individuals could shape their own destinies and contribute to the betterment of society.

Sir Thomas More was deeply embedded in the humanist circles of his time. A close friend of Desiderius Erasmus, one of the leading humanists and thinkers of the Renaissance, More was influenced by the latter's works and ideals. Erasmus's calls for religious reform and intellectual freedom resonated with More, shaping his thoughts on societal improvement and governance. More's education and career further immersed him in humanist thought. He studied at Oxford University, where he was exposed to classical texts and the writings of contemporary humanists. As a lawyer, judge, and eventually Lord Chancellor of England, More's professional life was marked by a commitment to justice, ethical governance, and intellectual rigor—all hallmarks of the humanist ethos.

## Utopia as a Humanist Work

Utopia reflects the ideals and concerns of Renaissance humanism in several key ways. The book is structured as a dialogue, a classical form of philosophical writing that encourages critical thinking and debate. This format allows More to explore complex social, political, and ethical issues through the character of Raphael Hythloday, a traveler who describes the ideal society of Utopia.

## The Value of Human Beings

One of the central tenets of humanism is the inherent value of human beings. In Utopia, More presents a society that prioritizes the well-being and dignity of its citizens. The Utopians live in a community where resources are shared, education is accessible to all, and labor is organized for the common good. This reflects the humanist belief in the potential for human improvement and the importance of creating conditions that allow individuals to flourish.

## The Pursuit of Knowledge

Education and the pursuit of knowledge are crucial elements of Utopian society. All citizens are encouraged to engage in intellectual pursuits, and the state supports a comprehensive system of education. This emphasis on learning mirrors the Renaissance humanists' advocacy for education as a means of personal and societal development. More's Utopians value reason and rational discourse, embodying the humanist ideal of an informed and thoughtful citizenry.

## Critique of Contemporary Society

More uses the fictional society of Utopia to critique the social, economic, and political conditions of 16th-century Europe. The issues he addresses, such as the misuse of power, social inequality, and the injustices of the legal system, are presented through the lens of humanist thought. By contrasting Utopia with the flawed realities of his own society, More encourages readers to question existing institutions and consider the possibilities for reform and improvement.

## Themes and Structure

Utopia is divided into two books. The first book sets the stage by presenting a critical discussion of European society, focusing on issues such as the misuse of power, social inequality, and the injustices of the legal and economic systems. More, through the character of Hythloday, critiques the enclosures in England, which displaced peasant farmers, and the harsh penalties for theft, arguing that these practices exacerbated poverty and crime.

In contrast, the second book describes the island of Utopia, a society characterized by communal ownership, rational governance, and social harmony. The Utopians live by a set of principles that emphasize equality, education, and the common good. Private property is abolished, and goods are stored in communal warehouses, where citizens take what they need. This system, Hythloday argues, eliminates poverty and reduces crime, as there is no incentive for theft or greed.

Education and rational discourse are highly valued in Utopia. All citizens are encouraged to engage in intellectual pursuits, and the society is governed by philosopher-kings who prioritize the well-being of the populace. Religious tolerance is another key aspect of Utopian society, reflecting More's humanist belief in the importance of individual conscience and moral reasoning.

He highlights the injustices that result from private property, the unequal distribution of wealth, and the corrupt nature of government and legal systems. The depiction of Utopia, where property is communal, and laws are simple and just, serves as a contrast to the flaws More sees in European governance. The Utopians live in a society where the government works for the common good, laws are designed to be easily understood by all, and the welfare of the people is prioritized above all else. This idealized society reflects More’s vision of what a good government and just laws might look like, emphasizing the need for reform in real-world governments.

## The Case for Reform

More’s Utopia suggests that reform is necessary when governments and laws are corrupt or fail to serve the public good. The book implicitly argues that people have a responsibility to seek reform when faced with such conditions. Hythloday, through his descriptions, illustrates how Utopia’s success stems from its just and equitable laws and governance. The contrast with European societies emphasizes the argument that reforming bad governments and laws is essential to achieving a more just and humane society.

More’s critique is not merely theoretical; it is a call to action. He suggests that it is possible to create a better society by addressing the root causes of injustice, such as the accumulation of wealth in the hands of a few, the exploitation of the poor, and the corruption of legal and political systems. By portraying Utopia as a society where these issues have been resolved, More offers a model for reformers to follow.

Methods of Reform

Utopia also provides insight into how reforms might be implemented. The Utopians, for instance, have designed their society to prevent the emergence of the very problems that plague European governments. For example, their communal ownership of property eliminates greed and the social divisions caused by wealth inequality. Their simple and transparent legal system ensures that laws are not manipulated by the powerful to exploit the weak.

From these examples, one can infer that More advocates for systemic change rather than piecemeal reforms. He seems to suggest that to reform a bad government or set of laws, one must address the underlying structures that allow corruption and injustice to thrive. This could involve radical changes to property laws, legal systems, and governance structures.

More’s Utopia emphasizes the importance of moral and ethical leadership. The Utopians are governed by wise and virtuous leaders who prioritize the common good over personal gain. This implies that successful reform requires leaders who are committed to justice and willing to challenge entrenched interests. Without such leadership, even the best-intentioned reforms may fail.

The Role of the Citizen

Another critical aspect of More’s argument is the role of the citizen in reforming bad governments and laws. Utopia suggests that citizens must be active participants in the political process and vigilant in holding their leaders accountable. The Utopians are deeply involved in their society's governance, and this active engagement helps prevent the abuses of power that are common in European societies.

More implies that reform is not solely the responsibility of leaders; it requires the active involvement of the people. Citizens must be educated, informed, and willing to demand change when necessary. This idea resonates with modern democratic principles, where an engaged and informed citizenry is seen as essential to the functioning of a healthy democracy.

## Challenges to Reform

While Utopia presents an optimistic vision of what a reformed society might look like, More is also aware of the challenges involved in achieving such reforms. Throughout the dialogue, Hythloday expresses skepticism about the possibility of implementing Utopian ideas in Europe, given the entrenched power of the ruling elites and the resistance to change.

More acknowledges that reform is difficult and may encounter significant opposition. By highlighting the stark contrast between Utopia and European society, he reinforces the idea that reform is not only necessary but possible. The very existence of Utopia as a model suggests that a better society can be imagined and, with effort, realized.

Sir Thomas More's Utopia presents a compelling argument for the need to reform bad governments and laws. By contrasting the idealized society of Utopia with the flawed governments of Europe, More makes a powerful case for systemic change. He suggests that such reforms require addressing the root causes of injustice, implementing radical changes to social and legal structures, and ensuring that leaders are committed to the common good. Utopia emphasizes the importance of active citizen participation in the political process. While More acknowledges the challenges involved in reform, he ultimately presents an optimistic vision of what can be achieved through thoughtful and determined efforts to create a more just and equitable society.

## Scholarly Interpretations

Scholars have offered various interpretations of Utopia, often debating More's intentions and the feasibility of his ideal society. Some view Utopia as a genuine proposal for social reform, while others see it as a satirical work, critiquing the impracticality of such ideals in the real world.

Quentin Skinner, in his analysis, suggests that Utopia is a complex blend of satire and earnest social critique. Skinner argues that More uses the fictional society to highlight the flaws of European governance while also provoking readers to think critically about the possibility of political and social improvement (Skinner, 2002). Skinner, highlights how Utopia embodies the humanist critique of contemporary governance and the aspiration for a more rational and just society (Skinner, 2002).

Stephen Greenblatt, in his study of Renaissance self-fashioning, emphasizes More's engagement with humanist ideals, particularly the emphasis on reason, education, and moral philosophy (Greenblatt, 1980). Greenblatt interprets Utopia through the lens of Renaissance humanism. He contends that Utopia reflects More's deep concern with the ethical dimensions of political life and his hope for a more just and rational society (Greenblatt, 1980).

These interpretations emphasize the extent to which Utopia is a product of its time, reflecting the intellectual currents and debates of the Renaissance. More's vision of an ideal society is deeply rooted in humanist principles, offering both a critique of his contemporary world and a hopeful blueprint for the future.

Sir Thomas More's Utopia is a quintessential work of Renaissance humanism. It reflects the era's emphasis on the value of human beings, the pursuit of knowledge, and the potential for societal improvement. More's engagement with humanist ideals is evident in his portrayal of an ideal society that prioritizes education, rational governance, and the common good. As a critique of contemporary society and a visionary work, Utopia continues to resonate with readers and scholars, offering timeless insights into the human condition and the possibilities for creating a better world.

Utopia has had a lasting impact on political thought and literature. The term utopia has entered the lexicon as a representation of an ideal society, and More's work continues to inspire debates about the nature of justice, equality, and human flourishing. The book's influence can be seen in various subsequent works of utopian and dystopian literature, such as Francis Bacon's New Atlantis and George Orwell's 1984.

More's exploration of communal ownership and social welfare has also resonated with various political movements, including socialism and communism. Although Utopia predates these ideologies, its critique of private property and advocacy for the common good align with later socialist thought.

Sir Thomas More's Utopia remains a profound and thought-provoking work that challenges readers to reflect on the nature of society and the possibilities for creating a more just and equitable world. Through its rich ideas and its innovative dialectical format, Utopia offers both a critique of 16th-century Europe and a visionary blueprint for an ideal society. As scholars continue to study and interpret Utopia, the book's relevance endures, offering timeless insights into the human quest for a better world.

Utopian visions often reflect the aspirations and anxieties of their times. In the wake of industrialization, thinkers like Karl Marx envisioned a classless society free from exploitation, while others, such as Adam Smith, championed the idea of a self-regulating market that would lead to prosperity for all. These visions are not mere fantasies but serve as critical reflections on existing societal structures and as blueprints for potential social and economic futures.

## The Historical Context of Economic Ideologies

To understand the evolution of socialism, communism, and capitalism, it is essential to research their historical contexts. Capitalism, as an economic system, emerged during the 16th century with the rise of mercantilism and later matured with the Industrial Revolution. Its development was marked by significant technological advancements and a shift from agrarian economies to industrial ones. Capitalist ideology is grounded in the works of classical economists such as Adam Smith, whose seminal work The Wealth of Nations (1776) laid the foundation for free market economics.

Socialism and communism, on the other hand, arose as critiques of the capitalist system. The 19th century saw the rise of industrial capitalism, which led to significant social inequalities and labor exploitation. In response, Karl Marx and Friedrich Engels published The Communist Manifesto in 1848, advocating for a revolutionary overthrow of capitalist societies to establish a classless, stateless society where the means of production are communally owned. This historical context is crucial for understanding the philosophical underpinnings and the ideological battles that have shaped modern economic thought.

## Philosophical Foundations and Misinterpretations

The philosophical foundations of socialism, communism, and capitalism are deeply intertwined with notions of justice, equality, and freedom. Capitalism is often associated with individual liberty and economic efficiency, emphasizing the role of self-interest and competition in driving innovation and wealth creation. Critics argue that unregulated capitalism leads to significant social inequalities and environmental degradation, as seen in the works of scholars like Thomas Piketty in Capital in the Twenty-First Century (2013).

Socialism and communism, by contrast, prioritize collective welfare and seek to eliminate the alleged disparities created by capitalist systems. Marxist theory, for instance, critiques the capitalist mode of production for its inherent exploitation of the working class (proletariat) by the owning class (bourgeoisie). The implementation of socialist and communist policies in various countries has often led to authoritarian regimes and economic inefficiencies, leading to widespread misinterpretations and criticisms of these ideologies.

A key philosophical debate revolves around the feasibility of achieving a utopian society through these economic systems. Utopian socialism, as proposed by early thinkers like Henri de Saint-Simon and Charles Fourier, envisioned a harmonious society achieved through moral and social reform rather than political revolution. Marxists argue that only through a revolutionary transformation can true socialism be realized.

Despite these differences, there is a possibility that the perfect form of capitalism, characterized by fair competition and innovation, shares similarities with the ideal form of communism, where resources are distributed based on contribution and need rather than profit. This opportunity for convergence suggests that the true barrier to utopia lies not in the ideological differences but in the practical challenges of human interference, misinterpretations, corruption, and greed.

The ideological divide between capitalism and communism has long been a source of contention in political and economic discourse. Despite their apparent differences, both systems share underlying principles that aim to maximize human welfare and societal well- being. The perfect form of capitalism, characterized by fair competition and innovation, aligns closely with the ideal form of communism, where resources are distributed based on contribution and need rather than profit.

At their core, both capitalism and communism strive for the organized and equitable allocation of resources, though they propose different mechanisms to achieve this goal. Ideal capitalism envisions a system where free markets drive innovation and efficiency, and competition ensures that resources are allocated to their most productive uses. In such a system, businesses and individuals are rewarded based on their contributions to economic growth and societal progress.

Similarly, the ideal form of communism aims to distribute resources based on individuals' contributions and needs, eliminating the profit motive and the resulting inequalities. In this system, the collective ownership of resources and means of production ensures that everyone has access to the necessities of life, promoting social welfare and reducing disparities. The convergence between the perfect forms of capitalism and communism lies in their mutual emphasis on fairness and contribution-based resource distribution. Both systems seek to create an environment where individuals can thrive based on their efforts and talents, and where societal resources are utilized in a manner that benefits all members of the community.

In ideal capitalism, this is achieved through mechanisms such as transparent markets, regulatory frameworks that prevent monopolies, and social safety nets that support those in need. In communism, the same principles are realized through collective decision-making processes, communal ownership, and the elimination of exploitative practices. When stripped of their ideological rhetoric, both systems advocate for a society where fairness, innovation, and the common good are paramount.

Alasdair MacIntyre, a prominent philosopher known for his contributions to moral and political philosophy, offers a nuanced perspective on this divide. His analysis transcends the conventional binaries of capitalism and communism, probing into the ethical foundations and practical implications of each system.

Capitalism and the Erosion of Virtue

MacIntyre's critique of capitalism is rooted in his broader philosophical project, which centers on the loss of a coherent moral tradition in modern society. In his seminal work, After Virtue, MacIntyre argues that capitalism, as an economic system, is intrinsically linked to the fragmentation of moral discourse. He contends that capitalism promotes individualism and a market-driven conception of human relations, which undermines the cultivation of virtues necessary for a flourishing community.

According to MacIntyre, capitalism reduces human interactions to transactions, where the pursuit of self-interest and profit maximization becomes the primary objective. This, in turn, leads to a society where moral considerations are subordinated to economic efficiency. The result is a disconnection between individuals and the communal practices that historically provided a framework for moral development. In this sense, capitalism, for MacIntyre, is not merely an economic system but a mode of life that erodes the possibility of achieving the common good.

Communism and the Promise of Collective Virtue

On the other hand, MacIntyre's engagement with communism is more ambivalent. While he is critical of the totalitarian manifestations of communism seen in the 20th century, he acknowledges that the ideology, in its ideal form, attempts to address some of the moral failings of capitalism. Communism, according to its proponents, seeks to establish a classless society where the means of production are collectively owned, and wealth is distributed according to need. This vision aligns with MacIntyre's emphasis on community and the common good.

MacIntyre is cautious about the implementation of communism, particularly the authoritarian methods used to achieve its goals. He argues that any political or economic system that undermines individual autonomy and fails to foster genuine moral practices is bound to replicate the moral failures of capitalism. Therefore, while communism theoretically holds the promise of a more virtuous society, its practical applications have often fallen short, leading to new forms of oppression and alienation.

This divide encompasses not just differences in economic systems but also fundamentally opposing views on human nature, social justice, and the role of the state. Mark Redhead, a political theorist known for his work on political ideologies and the ethics of political engagement, provides a distinctive analysis of this divide.

His exploration of the subject goes beyond mere economic or political arguments, delving into the philosophical and ethical dimensions that underpin the capitalist-communist dichotomy.

Capitalism: Freedom and Inequality

Redhead situates his critique of capitalism within the broader context of liberal thought, which often justifies capitalism on the grounds of promoting individual freedom and economic efficiency (Redhead, 2014). Redhead argues that capitalism's emphasis on individualism and market competition leads to significant social and economic inequalities. Redhead's analysis highlights the systemic nature of inequality in capitalist societies, where wealth and power become increasingly concentrated.

Redhead critiques the cultural impact of capitalism, arguing that it commodifies human relationships and undermines community values (Redhead, 2014). This perspective aligns with Redhead's (2014) findings that capitalism fosters a transactional view of social interactions, reducing human connections to mere economic exchanges.

Communism: Equality and Tyranny

In contrast, Redhead examines communism as a response to the inequalities perpetuated by capitalism. Communism's commitment to creating a classless society appeals to those who seek to address economic and social injustices (Redhead, 2014). Redhead is critical of the authoritarian tendencies observed in historical implementations of communism. Redhead (2014) argues that the centralization of power in communist regimes often leads to the suppression of individual freedoms and the emergence of new forms of domination.

Redhead's critique also extends to the ethical challenges of communism, particularly the tension between collective goals and individual rights (Redhead, 2014). This analysis is supported by research which underscores the difficulties of achieving true equality without compromising personal autonomy.

## Bridging the Divide: A Call for Ethical Pluralism

Redhead's analysis ultimately points to the need for a more nuanced approach to political and economic theory… one that transcends the binary opposition between capitalism and communism. He advocates for ethical pluralism, a concept that recognizes the validity of multiple moral perspectives and seeks to balance freedom, equality, and community (Redhead, 2014).

This approach resonates with the argument that ideological rigidity hinders the development of more just and sustainable systems. Redhead's call for ethical pluralism challenges us to consider how the strengths of both capitalism and communism can be integrated into a more humane and equitable framework for organizing society. Mark Redhead offers a critical examination of the ideological divide between capitalism and communism, highlighting the ethical and practical shortcomings of both systems. His advocacy for ethical pluralism invites a rethinking of political and economic systems in ways that prioritize human dignity, moral complexity, and social justice.

## The Need for a Moral and Political Synthesis

MacIntyre and Redhead's analysis of the ideological divide between capitalism and communism ultimately points to the need for a moral and political synthesis that transcends the limitations of both systems. They advocate for a return to Aristotelian ethics and an ethical pluralism, where the focus is on the development of virtues within a community context. In this framework, economic systems are evaluated not merely by their efficiency or productivity but by their ability to support the moral development of individuals and the community.

## Practical Challenges: Human Interference, Corruption, and Greed

Despite the theoretical convergence of capitalism and communism, the practical implementation of these ideals has been marred by human interference and limitations to their optimization. In capitalist systems, unregulated markets can lead to monopolistic practices, economic disparities, and exploitation. Wealth concentration and corporate influence often undermine the principles of fair competition and equal opportunity. Communist regimes, on the other hand, have historically struggled with bureaucratic inefficiencies, lack of incentives for innovation, and authoritarian governance. The centralization of power and resources has frequently resulted in corruption and abuse, deviating from the original ideals of equality and communal welfare.

## Overcoming Practical Challenges

To move closer to a utopian society that harmonizes the best elements of capitalism and communism, it is crucial to address these practical challenges. This requires the development of institutional frameworks that ensure transparency, accountability, and ethical governance. Technology, particularly blockchain and digital contracts, can play a significant role in creating systems that minimize corruption and promote fair resource distribution.

Blockchain technology, for instance, offers a decentralized and immutable ledger system that can improve transparency in both capitalist and communist frameworks. By enabling secure and transparent transactions, blockchain can reduce opportunities for corruption and ensure that contributions are accurately recorded and rewarded. Digital contracts can enforce fair exchanges and prevent exploitation, promoting a system that reflects the interests of all rather than a select few.

The convergence between the perfect forms of capitalism and communism highlights the shared principles of fairness, contribution-based resource distribution, and societal well-being. The true barrier to achieving a utopian society lies not in the ideological differences between these systems but in the practical challenges of human interference, corruption, and greed. By leveraging technology and developing smart institutional frameworks, we can overcome these obstacles and move closer to realizing a society where innovation, fairness, and the common good are prioritized.

References


- Greenblatt, Stephen. (1980). Renaissance Self-Fashioning: From More to Shakespeare. University of Chicago Press.
- More, Thomas. (1516).Utopia.
- Marx, Karl, and Friedrich Engels. (1848) The Communist Manifesto.
- More, Thomas. (1516). Utopia.
- Piketty, Thomas. (2013). Capital in the Twenty-First Century.
- Redhead, Mark. (2014). Reasoning With Who We Are: Democratic Theory For a Not So Liberal Era.
- Skinner, Quentin. (2002). The Foundations of Modern Political Thought: Volume 1, The Renaissance. Cambridge University Press.
- Smith, Adam. (1776). The Wealth of Nations.

## Chapter 1: The Philosophical Underpinnings of Economic Systems

### Historical Context and Misinterpretations

Economic systems have evolved significantly over centuries, shaped by historical contexts and human experiences. Capitalism, socialism, and communism, as dominant economic ideologies, have each emerged in response to specific socio-economic conditions and philosophical debates. The prominence of capitalism, socialism, and communism as the main economic and social systems of the last few centuries can be attributed to their strong theoretical foundations and the specific historical contexts in which they arose. Capitalism's emphasis on individual liberty and market efficiency, socialism's focus on collective welfare and social justice, and communism's vision of a classless society have each resonated with different socio-economic conditions and philosophical debates. Understanding the reasons behind the rise of these systems provides valuable insights into their impacts on human history and their continuing relevance in contemporary debates about economic and social organization.

### Ancient Ideas about Capitalism

Capitalism, characterized by private property, market exchange, and profit motive, finds its rudimentary elements in ancient economies, particularly in Greece and Rome.

### Ancient Greece

In ancient Greece, economic thought was significantly influenced by philosophers like Aristotle and Xenophon.

- Aristotle (384-322 BCE): Aristotle's works, particularly Politics and Nicomachean Ethics, discuss the role of property and wealth in society. He distinguished between oikonomia (household management) and chrematistics (the art of acquiring wealth). Aristotle viewed chrematistics skeptically, believing that the pursuit of wealth for its own sake was unnatural and could lead to moral corruption. He acknowledged the necessity of private property for the stability and prosperity of the household and the polis (Aristotle, Politics, Book I).

- Xenophon (431-354 BCE): Xenophon, in his work Oeconomicus, explores the management of household economies and estates. His writings reflect early capitalist practices, emphasizing efficiency, productivity, and the benefits of skillful management (Xenophon, Oeconomicus).
- Plato (428-348 BCE): In the Republic, Plato proposed that the guardian class should live communally, without private property or family ties, to prevent conflicts of interest and ensure their focus on the common good. This idea aligns with socialist principles of collective ownership and equality (Plato, Republic, Book V).

Aristotle: The Ethics and Economics of Private Property

Aristotle, one of the most influential ancient philosophers, had a nuanced view of economics, which he detailed in his works Politics and Nicomachean Ethics. He made a clear distinction between what he saw as natural and unnatural forms of wealth acquisition.

Argument for Private Property

Aristotle argued that private property was natural and beneficial for several reasons. He believed it promoted responsibility and diligence, as people are more likely to take care of and improve what they own. In Politics, he stated:

Property should be in a sense common, but, as a general rule, private; for, when everyone has a distinct interest, men will not complain of one another, and they will make more progress, because every one will be attending to his own business (Aristotle, Politics, Book II, 1263a).

Aristotle's support for private property laid the groundwork for later capitalist thought, emphasizing individual responsibility and the efficient use of resources.

Critique of Wealth Accumulation

Aristotle was critical of wealth accumulation for its own sake, which he considered unnatural. He distinguished between oikonomia (household management) and chrematistics (wealth acquisition). While the former was necessary and honorable, the latter was seen as potentially corrupting. He warned against the pursuit of money beyond what is needed for a good life:

The life of money-making is one undertaken by compulsion, and wealth is evidently not the good we are seeking; for it is merely useful and for the sake of something else (Aristotle, Nicomachean Ethics, Book I, 1096a).

Xenophon: Practical Economics and Estate Management

Xenophon, a contemporary of Plato, offered a more practical perspective on economics, particularly in his work Oeconomicus, which discusses household management and estate efficiency.

Argument for Efficient Management

Xenophon's contributions to economic thought were pragmatic, focusing on the effective management of estates and resources. He emphasized the importance of skillful management and the benefits of a well-ordered household economy. In Oeconomicus, he wrote:

He who by the help of his knowledge gains an estate, which will give him the means of a liberal support, and further, enables him to benefit his friends and to serve his country, appears to me to be the best and the most useful citizen (Xenophon, Oeconomicus, VII).

Xenophon's emphasis on efficiency and productivity aligns with early capitalist principles, advocating for the diligent management of resources to achieve prosperity.

## Plato: The Ideal of Communal Living

Plato, Aristotle's teacher, had a contrasting view on economic systems, particularly regarding private property and communal living. His work The Republic outlines his vision of an ideal state, where he advocates for the abolition of private property among the guardian class.

### Argument for Communal Property

Plato believed that private property led to social strife and inequality. In his ideal state, the guardian class, responsible for ruling, would have no private possessions. Instead, they would live communally to prevent conflicts of interest and ensure their focus on the common good. He argued:

They will possess no private property, but only communal property; they will live in common and will share their possessions in common (Plato, Republic, Book III, 416d).

Plato's vision aimed to eliminate the sources of corruption and conflict, promoting unity and shared purpose among the ruling class. This early form of socialism sought to create a harmonious and just society through communal living and shared resources.

### Critique of Private Property

Plato criticized private property for fostering greed and division. He believed that the desire for personal wealth detracted from the common good and led to social instability:

The citizens of our state must be watched over, and the greatest watch must be kept upon those who have been made rulers. These are the men who will do the greatest harm to the state, if they become bad, and the greatest benefit, if they are good (Plato, Republic, Book III, 416a).

Ancient Greek philosophers provided a rich set of arguments for and against different economic systems, laying the foundations for future economic thought. Aristotle's support for private property and critique of excessive wealth accumulation, Plato's advocacy for communal living and his critique of private property, and Xenophon's practical approach to estate management each offer valuable insights into the ancient debate on economic systems. These philosophical discourses continue to impact and influence contemporary discussions on the best ways to organize economic life and achieve social justice.

Ancient Rome

The Roman Empire exhibited significant commercial activities and practices that align with capitalist principles.

- Roman Law and Property Rights: Roman law codified private property rights, facilitating trade, contracts, and economic transactions. The legal framework supported a market economy where individuals could accumulate and transfer wealth (Buckland, 1939).
- Cato the Elder (234-149 BCE): In his work De Agricultura, Cato the Elder provided practical advice on estate management, emphasizing profitability and efficient use of resources. His approach reflects an early form of agrarian capitalism (Cato the Elder, De Agricultura).

The Parable of the Talents in Matthew 25: An Inspiration for Capitalism

The Parable of the Talents, found in Matthew 25:14-30, is one of the most well-known teachings of Jesus in the New Testament. This parable has been subject to various interpretations throughout history, with some scholars arguing that it provides a moral and theological foundation for the principles of capitalism.

In the Parable of the Talents, a master entrusts his property to his servants before leaving on a journey. He gives five talents to one servant, two talents to another, and one talent to the third, each according to their ability. Upon his return, the master asks for an account of how they have used his property. The servants who received five and two talents respectively report that they have doubled the money through trade, while the servant who received one talent admits he buried it out of fear. The master praises the industrious servants and rewards them but rebukes the fearful servant and casts him into outer darkness.

Interpretations and Economic Implications Encouragement of Enterprise and Investment

The parable emphasizes the importance of using one's resources wisely and taking initiative to generate wealth. Scholars like Craig Blomberg argue that the parable emphasizes the value of diligence and entrepreneurial spirit (Blomberg, 1990). The master's praise of the servants who invested and multiplied their talents can be seen as a commendation of productive investment and risk-taking, key components of capitalist economies.

Reward for Productivity

The servants who successfully doubled their talents are rewarded with greater responsibilities and increased wealth, reflecting the capitalist principle that hard work and productivity should be rewarded. This idea is central to the meritocratic aspect of capitalism, where individuals are incentivized to work hard and innovate because their efforts can lead to economic success and upward mobility.

Condemnation of Idleness

The third servant, who buried his talent, is condemned for his inaction and fear. This part of the parable aligns with capitalist critiques of idleness and the importance of active participation in the economy. In a capitalist framework, capital that is not put to productive use is considered wasted potential, which can hinder economic growth and prosperity.

Scholarly Perspectives Historical and Cultural Context

Scholars such as Richard H. Hiers emphasize understanding the parable within its historical and cultural context. In the first-century Mediterranean world, the concept of investment and the use of money for generating profit were well understood (Hiers, 2004). By employing the familiar practice of entrusting money to servants for investment, Jesus used an economic activity that his audience could easily relate to, thereby imparting moral and spiritual lessons through economic principles.

Theological Implications

Theological interpretations of the parable often focus on the broader spiritual message rather than its economic implications. For instance, Klyne Snodgrass argues that the parable primarily teaches about the Kingdom of God and the responsible stewardship of the gifts and opportunities God provides (Snodgrass, 2008). The economic activities described in the parable serve as a metaphor for spiritual responsibilities, suggesting a positive view of enterprise and diligent work.

Capitalism and Christian Ethics

Max Weber's seminal work, The Protestant Ethic and the Spirit of Capitalism, looks at Protestant ethics, including the interpretation of biblical parables like that of the Talents, contributed to the development of capitalist attitudes (Weber, 1905). Weber argues that the emphasis on hard work, frugality, and economic success as signs of divine favor influenced the rise of capitalism in Western Europe. The Parable of the Talents, with its endorsement of productive use of resources and reward for diligent work, fits within this ethical framework.

The Parable of the Talents in Matthew 25:14-30 has been interpreted in various ways, but its implications for economic thought are particularly notable. The parable's emphasis on investment, productivity, and the condemnation of idleness are aligned with key principles of capitalism. Scholarly interpretations support the view that this parable, while primarily a theological and moral teaching, also provides a conceptual foundation for the values that underpin capitalist economies. Understanding the parable's influence on economic thought helps to illuminate the intersections between religious teachings and economic systems, revealing how ancient texts can inspire and justify contemporary economic practices.

## Ancient Ideas about Socialism

Socialism, with its emphasis on collective ownership and social welfare, can be traced to ancient practices and philosophical ideas advocating communal living and shared resources.

### Ancient Egypt

Ancient Egypt's centralized economy, where the state controlled significant resources, reflects early socialist principles.

- State Control and Redistribution: The pharaoh, as the divine ruler, owned all land and resources. The state collected and redistributed goods, ensuring that the population had access to food and essential services, particularly during times of scarcity (Kemp, 2006).

## Ancient Ideas about Communism

Communism, advocating for a classless, stateless society with communal ownership, finds its philosophical roots in early utopian visions.

### Early Christian Communities

Early Christian communities practiced forms of communal living that resemble communist ideals.

- Acts of the Apostles: The New Testament describes how early Christians in Jerusalem shared all possessions and resources, distributing them according to need. This practice aimed to create a community without poverty or inequality (Acts 2:44-45).

Zeno of Citium and Stoicism

Stoic philosophy, particularly the teachings of Zeno of Citium, founder of the Stoic school, contains elements that align with communist ideals.

- Zeno of Citium (334-262 BCE): Zeno's ideal society, as described in his work Republic, envisioned a community where people lived according to nature, without private property, money, or social hierarchies. This utopian vision emphasizes equality and communal living (Long, 1986).

The ancient antecedents of capitalism, socialism, and communism illustrate that ideas about economic organization and social justice have deep historical roots. Ancient Greece and Rome exhibited early capitalist practices through their emphasis on private property and market exchange. Socialism's focus on collective ownership and social welfare can be seen in the centralized economies of ancient Egypt and the philosophical writings of Plato. Communism's vision of a classless, communal society finds echoes in early Christian communities and Stoic philosophy. Understanding these ancient ideas provides valuable insights into the enduring human quest for economic systems that promote prosperity, equality, and social harmony.

Modern Capitalism

Capitalism, as an economic system, developed in the 16th century alongside the rise of mercantilism and later matured during the Industrial Revolution. Capitalism began to take shape during the late Middle Ages and the early Renaissance. Mercantilism, a form of economic nationalism that emphasized the accumulation of wealth through trade and colonization helped shape capitalistic ideals. It was during the Industrial Revolution of the 18th and 19th centuries that capitalism fully matured as a distinct economic system.

Early proponents like Adam Smith, in his seminal work The Wealth of Nations (1776), advocated for a system where free markets, driven by individual self-interest and competition, would lead to wealth creation and total societal prosperity. Smith's invisible hand theory posits that individual pursuits can unintentionally benefit society at large, promoting efficiency and innovation (Smith, 1776). John Locke (1632-1704) was also a major contributor to early capitalistic ideas. Locke's theory of property, articulated in his Second Treatise of Government (1689), argues that individuals have a natural right to own property through their labor. This notion of private property as a natural right became a cornerstone of capitalist ideology (Locke, 1689).

## Historical Context

The Industrial Revolution brought about significant technological advancements and shifts in production processes. The transition from agrarian economies to industrialized ones led to the creation of new markets and the accumulation of capital. Adam Smith, often regarded as the father of modern economics, laid the intellectual foundation for capitalism in his seminal work, The Wealth of Nations (1776). Smith argued that individuals pursuing their self-interest would inadvertently contribute to the general good of society through a self-regulating market mechanism, which he famously termed the invisible hand (Smith, 1776).

## Philosophical Debates

Capitalism is grounded in the principles of private property, free markets, and competition. Proponents argue that these elements drive innovation, efficiency, and economic growth. Critics have pointed out the system's tendency to generate economic inequalities and social injustices. Karl Marx, in particular, critiqued capitalism for its inherent exploitation of the working class (proletariat) by the owning class (bourgeoisie). Marx's analysis of capitalism's contradictions laid the groundwork for the development of socialist and communist ideologies (Marx & Engels, 1848).

Despite its successes, capitalism has faced significant criticisms and misinterpretations. The unregulated capitalist system has often resulted in economic disparities, social inequalities, and environmental degradation. Critics like Karl Marx argued that capitalism inherently leads to the exploitation of the working class by the owning class, resulting in class struggles and social unrest (Marx & Engels, 1848).

Socialism and Communism

Socialism and communism arose as counterpoints to capitalism, aiming to address its perceived failures. Socialism advocates for collective ownership of resources and means of production, seeking to reduce inequalities through redistribution. The philosophy behind socialism emphasizes social welfare and communal responsibility.

Socialism emerged as a response to the social and economic inequalities exacerbated by industrial capitalism. It advocates for collective ownership of the means of production and the distribution of resources based on need rather than profit.

The historical roots of socialism are linked to the labor movements of the 19th century and the rise of socialist political parties.

- Jean-Jacques Rousseau (1712-1778): In his work The Social Contract (1762), Rousseau argued for a society where individuals collectively make decisions for the common good. His ideas on equality and collective governance influenced early socialist thought (Rousseau, 1762).
- Labor Movements (19th century): The industrialization era saw the rise of labor unions and movements advocating for workers' rights, fair wages, and improved working conditions. These movements laid the

groundwork for socialist political activism (Hobsbawm, 1964).

- Rise of Socialist Parties (late 19th-early 20th centuries): Socialist parties emerged in Europe, advocating for the redistribution of wealth, social welfare programs, and the nationalization of key industries. The establishment of the Socialist International in 1889 facilitated the spread of socialist ideas globally (Hobsbawm, 1987).

The 19th century saw the rise of labor movements and socialist thought, fueled by the harsh working conditions and economic disparities of the industrial era. Thinkers like Robert Owen and Charles Fourier proposed early socialist models that emphasized cooperative living and shared ownership.

Philosophical Debates

Socialist theory is rooted in the belief that collective ownership and democratic control of resources can lead to a more equitable and just society. While some forms of socialism advocate for gradual reform within existing political systems, others, like Marxism, call for radical transformation. Critics of socialism argue that it can lead to inefficiencies, lack of incentives for innovation, and potential authoritarianism. The practical implementation of socialism has varied widely, from democratic socialism in Scandinavia to the more centralized models seen in the Soviet Union and other communist states.

Communism, as articulated by Karl Marx and Friedrich Engels in The Communist Manifesto (1848), envisions a classless, stateless society where the means of production are communally owned. Marx and Engels argued that capitalism's contradictions would inevitably lead to its downfall and the rise of a communist society, where resources are distributed based on need and contribution rather than profit (Marx & Engels, 1848). Communism, as envisioned by Marx and Engels, represents the most radical form of socialism. It seeks to eliminate private property and establish a classless society where resources are distributed based on need. The publication of The Communist Manifesto marked a significant turning point in socialist thought, advocating for a revolutionary overthrow of capitalist systems to establish a classless, stateless society (Marx & Engels, 1848).

## Historical Context

The Russian Revolution of 1917 and the subsequent establishment of the Soviet Union marked the first large-scale attempt to implement communist principles. Under the leadership of Vladimir Lenin and later Joseph Stalin, the Soviet Union pursued policies of collectivization and central planning. These efforts aimed to eliminate class distinctions and create a stateless, communist society. The practical realities of governance, economic management, and political control led to significant deviations from Marxist ideals (Fitzpatrick, 1994).

The vision of communism, as articulated by Marx and Engels, promised a revolutionary transformation of society through the abolition of private property, the establishment of a classless society, and the communal ownership of the means of production. Communism was intended to resolve the inherent contradictions of capitalism, particularly the exploitation of the proletariat by the bourgeoisie. The ultimate aim was to create a society where wealth and power were equitably distributed, ensuring that all individuals could achieve their full potential without the constraints of class oppression (Marx & Engels, 1848).

Throughout the 20th century, various countries attempted to realize this vision, leading to the establishment of communist states. In the $20^{th}$ century, communism spread to various parts of the world, particularly in Eastern Europe, Asia, and Latin America, often through revolutionary movements and wars of independence. The Chinese Revolution (1949) and the Cuban Revolution (1959) were significant events that established communist regimes in these regions (Service, 2007).

Historical Establishments of Communism The Soviet Union

The Soviet Union, established after the Bolshevik Revolution of 1917, was the first major attempt to implement Marxist principles on a national scale. Under Vladimir Lenin and later Joseph Stalin, the Soviet government pursued policies of rapid industrialization, collectivization of agriculture, and centralized economic planning.

Critiques:

- Economic Inefficiency: Scholars such as Alec Nove have argued that the Soviet command economy was marked by significant inefficiencies, including misallocation of resources, lack of innovation, and bureaucratic red tape (Nove, 1983). Central planning often failed to respond adequately to consumer needs and market signals, leading to chronic shortages and surpluses.
- Political Repression: The Stalinist period was characterized by severe political repression, including purges, forced labor camps (Gulags), and widespread surveillance. Robert Conquest's The Great Terror documents the extent of state violence and the elimination of perceived political opponents (Conquest, 1990).
- Lack of Political Freedom: The centralization of power in the Communist Party led to the suppression of political dissent and the elimination of democratic processes. Scholars such as Stephen F. Cohen have noted that this concentration of power undermined the potential for genuine socialist democracy (Cohen, 1974).

Maoist China

Following the Chinese Revolution of 1949, Mao Zedong established the People's Republic of China, implementing Marxist-Leninist principles adapted to Chinese conditions. Key policies included land reforms, the collectivization of agriculture, and the promotion of heavy industry.

Critiques:

- The Great Leap Forward: This campaign aimed to rapidly industrialize China but resulted in one of the deadliest famines in history, with estimates of deaths ranging from 15 to 45 million. Scholars such as Frank Dikötter have attributed this disaster to misguided policies, forced collectivization, and unrealistic production targets (Dikötter, 2010).
- The Cultural Revolution: Initiated by Mao in 1966, the Cultural Revolution sought to reassert communist ideology by purging capitalist and traditional elements from Chinese society. This period was marked by widespread persecution, destruction of cultural heritage, and significant social upheaval. Historians like Roderick MacFarquhar have detailed the immense human and cultural costs of this movement (MacFarquhar, 1997).

Other Communist States

Other countries, including Cuba, North Korea, and various Eastern European nations, also attempted to establish communist systems. Each faced unique challenges and criticisms:

Cuba: While Cuba under Fidel Castro achieved significant improvements in healthcare and education, it also faced economic stagnation, political repression, and reliance on Soviet support. Samuel Farber's work critically assesses both the achievements and shortcomings of the Cuban Revolution (Farber, 2006).

- North Korea: The regime established by Kim Il-sung has been characterized by extreme authoritarianism, economic hardship, and isolationism. Scholars such as Bruce Cumings have examined the historical and political dynamics that have led to North Korea's current state (Cumings, 2004).
- Eastern Europe: The fall of communist regimes in Eastern Europe in 1989-1991 highlighted the systemic failures of these systems, including economic inefficiency, lack of political freedom, and widespread dissatisfaction among the populace. Timothy Garton Ash's accounts provide

detailed insights into the decline and collapse of these regimes (Garton Ash, 1990).

Theoretical and Practical Divergences

The establishment of communism in the modern world often diverged significantly from its theoretical ideals. Key issues include:

- Authoritarianism vs. Democracy: While Marx envisioned a proletarian democracy, most communist states became highly authoritarian. The concentration of power in the Communist Party led to the suppression of political pluralism and civil liberties.
- Economic Planning vs. Market Efficiency: Centralized economic planning, a hallmark of communist states, often resulted in inefficiencies and stagnation. Critics argue that the lack of market mechanisms stifled innovation and productivity, as documented by Janos Kornai in The Socialist System (Kornai, 1992).
- Ideological Rigidity vs. Practical Flexibility: Many communist regimes adhered rigidly to ideological orthodoxy, which hindered their ability to adapt to changing economic and social conditions. This rigidity often exacerbated existing problems rather than solving them.

The establishment of communism in the modern world presents a complex and multivariate picture. While communist states have achieved some social gains, such as improved literacy rates and healthcare access, they have also faced significant economic, political, and human rights challenges. The theoretical ideals of communism often clashed with the practical realities of governance, leading to outcomes that deviated sharply from the envisioned classless, stateless society. A critical examination of these experiences provides valuable lessons for understanding the potential and limitations of radical socio-economic transformations.

## Capitalism

Capitalism, as an economic system, developed in the 16th century alongside the rise of mercantilism and later matured during the Industrial Revolution. Early proponents like Adam Smith, in his seminal work The Wealth of Nations (1776), advocated for a system where free markets, driven by individual self-interest and competition, would lead to wealth creation and general societal prosperity. Smith's Invisible Hand theory posits that individual pursuits can unintentionally benefit society at large, promoting efficiency and innovation (Smith, 1776).

Despite its successes, capitalism has faced significant criticisms and misinterpretations. The unregulated capitalist system has often resulted in economic disparities, social inequalities, and environmental degradation. Critics like Karl Marx argued that capitalism inherently leads to the exploitation of the working class by the owning class, resulting in class struggles and social unrest (Marx & Engels, 1848).

## Socialism and Communism

Socialism and communism arose as counterpoints to capitalism, aiming to address its perceived failures. Socialism advocates for collective ownership of resources and means of production, seeking to reduce inequalities through redistribution. The philosophy behind socialism emphasizes social welfare and communal responsibility.

Communism, as articulated by Karl Marx and Friedrich Engels in The Communist Manifesto (1848), envisions a classless, stateless society where the means of production are communally owned. Marx and Engels argued that capitalism's contradictions would inevitably lead to its downfall and the rise of a communist society, where resources are distributed based on need and contribution rather than profit (Marx & Engels, 1848).

The implementation of socialist and communist ideologies in various countries has often led to authoritarian regimes, economic inefficiencies, and widespread corruption. These outcomes have fueled misinterpretations and skepticism about the feasibility of these systems in practice.

## Common Ground and Divergence

While capitalism, socialism, and communism are often seen as fundamentally opposed, they share common philosophical underpinnings and goals. All three ideologies strive for human welfare, societal well-being, and efficient resource allocation, though they propose different mechanisms to achieve these ends.

### Common Ground

At their core, both capitalism and communism emphasize the value of human effort and the importance of equitable resource distribution. Capitalism, in its ideal form, promotes meritocracy, where individuals are rewarded based on their contributions to economic growth and innovation. Similarly, communism advocates for a system where resources are distributed according to individuals' needs and contributions, ensuring that everyone has access to the essentials for a dignified life.

Both systems also recognize the potential for human improvement and the importance of creating conditions that allow individuals to thrive. Capitalist societies emphasize individual liberty and entrepreneurship, while communist societies focus on communal well-being and collective decision-making.

### Divergence

The primary divergence between these ideologies lies in their approach to ownership and production. Capitalism advocates for private ownership and market-driven economies, arguing that competition and self-interest drive innovation and efficiency. In contrast, communism calls for the abolition of private property and centralized planning, believing that communal ownership eliminates exploitation and ensures equitable resource distribution.

These differing approaches reflect deeper philosophical disagreements about human nature and the role of the state. Capitalists argue that individual freedom and market mechanisms are essential for progress, while communists believe that only through collective ownership and state intervention can true equality and social justice be achieved.

## Toward a Utopian Vision: Synthesis of Ideals

The pursuit of a utopian society requires synthesizing the best elements of both capitalist and communist ideologies. Such a society would prioritize fairness, innovation, and the common good, balancing individual liberty with communal responsibility.

### Contribution-Based System

A contribution-based system, where resources are allocated based on individuals' efforts and contributions, could bridge the gap between capitalism and communism. This approach emphasizes meritocracy while ensuring that basic needs are met for all members of society. Technological advancements, particularly in blockchain and digital contracts, offer tools to create transparent and fair systems for measuring and rewarding contributions.

The key to bridging the ideological gap between capitalism and communism lies in redefining the concept of value. In traditional capitalist systems, value is often equated with profit, while in communist systems, it is equated with utility and need. A contribution-based economic system would redefine value as a combination of these factors, emphasizing both the economic and social contributions of individuals. This redefinition allows for a more holistic view of economic activity, one that values both individual achievements and collective well-being. By doing so, it aligns the incentives of capitalism with the moral imperatives of socialism and communism, creating a system that is both just and efficient.

## Leveraging Technology

As society advances into an era increasingly defined by technology, there is a growing opportunity to synthesize the most beneficial aspects of these ideologies into a unified, contribution-based economic system. Such a system, underpinned by technological innovation, could bridge the gap between the meritocratic incentives of capitalism and the collective welfare goals of communism, creating a society where individual contributions are recognized, and basic needs are universally met.

### The Role of Technology in Redefining Value

In traditional capitalist economies, value is often measured by profit and market success, while in communist ideologies, value is tied to meeting basic human needs and achieving social equity (Piketty, 2014). Technology, particularly blockchain and artificial intelligence (AI), offers a new way to redefine value by making it possible to quantify and reward contributions to society more holistically (Tapscott & Tapscott, 2016).

Blockchain technology can be employed to create transparent and immutable records of individual contributions, whether they be economic, social, or environmental. This ledger-based system can ensure that contributions that might not traditionally be valued in a capitalist framework—such as community service or environmental stewardship—are recognized and rewarded (Swan, 2015). By using smart contracts, society can automate the distribution of rewards based on predefined metrics of social value, and aligning individual incentives with the broader good (Buterin, 2014). Blockchain technology, with its decentralized and immutable ledger system, can improve transparency and reduce opportunities for corruption. By securely recording transactions and contributions, blockchain can ensure that resources are distributed fairly and equitably. Digital contracts can enforce agreements and prevent exploitation, promoting a system that reflects the interests of the community as a whole.

AI can further improve this system by analyzing vast amounts of data to assess the impact of various contributions. For instance, AI algorithms can evaluate the long-term social and environmental benefits of certain actions, allowing for a more nuanced and equitable distribution of resources (Brynjolfsson & McAfee, 2014). This approach could mitigate some of the inequalities inherent in capitalist systems while avoiding the inefficiencies that have historically plagued centrally planned economies.

## Ensuring Basic Needs Through Technological Innovation

One of the central promises of communism is the provision of basic needs for all members of society, a goal that is often compromised by inefficiencies in resource allocation (Marx, 1867). In a contribution-based economic system powered by technology, ensuring basic needs could be more efficiently managed. For instance, AI can optimize the distribution of resources such as food, healthcare, and education, ensuring that they reach those in need with minimal waste and maximum impact (Russell & Norvig, 2020).

Technology can enable the creation of decentralized autonomous organizations (DAOs) that operate independently of human intervention to manage and distribute resources fairly (Wright & De Filippi, 2015). These organizations could be programmed to prioritize equitable access to essential services, thereby fulfilling the communist ideal of meeting basic human needs while maintaining the efficiency and innovation associated with capitalist economies.

## Meritocracy and Innovation in a Tech-Driven Economy

Capitalism's strength lies in its promotion of innovation and meritocracy, where individuals are rewarded based on their ability to create economic value (Schumpeter, 2008). In a contribution-based system, technology can preserve and even enhance this meritocratic principle by ensuring that rewards are distributed based on the true value of contributions to society, not just economic profitability.

For example, platforms that use AI to match individuals with opportunities based on their skills and the societal impact of their work can help foster a more inclusive and dynamic economy (Autor, 2015). Additionally, blockchain can ensure that intellectual property rights are protected and that creators are fairly compensated for their innovations, maintaining the incentive structures that drive progress in capitalist economies (Tapscott & Tapscott, 2016).

Technology holds the key to creating a contribution-based economic system that synthesizes the most important aspects of communism and capitalism. By leveraging blockchain and AI, society can redefine value in a way that rewards contributions to the common good, ensures that basic needs are met, and promotes innovation through a meritocratic system. This approach not only addresses the shortcomings of traditional economic systems but also offers a path toward a more just, efficient, and sustainable future.

## Overcoming Human Interference

The practical implementation of ideal economic systems faces significant challenges, primarily due to human interference, corruption, and greed. Both capitalist and communist societies have struggled with these issues, often deviating from their theoretical ideals. Despite their theoretical qualities, both capitalism and communism have encountered significant challenges in practice. One of the primary issues is human interference, which often manifests in the form of corruption, greed, and the concentration of power. In capitalist societies, the pursuit of profit can lead to monopolistic practices, income inequality, and exploitation, as seen in the rise of oligarchies and the influence of money in politics (Piketty, 2014). The capitalist ideal of free competition is frequently undermined by corporate lobbying, regulatory capture, and financial manipulation, resulting in a system that benefits the few at the expense of the many.

Communist societies, on the other hand, have struggled with issues of centralized control, bureaucratic inefficiency, and authoritarianism. The concentration of power in the hands of the state often leads to corruption and the suppression of individual freedoms (Orwell, 1945). The absence of market mechanisms can result in resource misallocation, shortages, and a lack of innovation, as evidenced by the economic stagnation in the former Soviet Union (Nove, 1983). The communist ideal of equality is often compromised by the emergence of a privileged ruling class, contradicting the very principles of the system.

The synthesis of capitalist and communist ideals offers a promising path toward a more just and effective economic system. By combining the strengths of both models—capitalism's dynamism and communism's commitment to equality—it is possible to create a system that better aligns with the realities of human nature and the complexities of modern society. Such a system would be better equipped to address the practical challenges of corruption, greed, and power concentration, ultimately leading to a more balanced and prosperous world.

## Ethical Governance

Developing institutional frameworks that ensure transparency, accountability, and ethical governance is crucial for overcoming these challenges. This involves creating systems that are resistant to corruption and capable of adapting to changing social and economic conditions. In contemporary societies, the challenges of corruption, lack of accountability, and opaque governance structures have posed significant threats to sustainable development and social justice. Developing institutional frameworks that ensure transparency, accountability, and ethical governance is crucial for overcoming these challenges. Such frameworks must be designed to resist corruption, adapt to changing social and economic conditions, and promote the long-term well-being of all citizens.

### The Importance of Transparency in Governance

Transparency is a cornerstone of ethical governance. It involves making government actions, decisions, and policies accessible to the public, allowing for informed citizen participation and scrutiny. Transparency reduces the opportunity for corruption by exposing government activities to public oversight and ensuring that decision-making processes are open to all stakeholders (Kolstad & Wiig, 2009).

In practical terms, transparency can be enhanced through the implementation of open data initiatives, where government agencies publish data on their operations, expenditures, and decision-making processes in an accessible and usable format. This enables civil society organizations, the media, and the general public to monitor government actions on all levels and hold officials accountable (Meijer, 2015). Transparency fosters trust between the government and its citizens, which is essential for the legitimacy and effectiveness of governance structures.

Accountability Mechanisms and Ethical Governance

Accountability is closely linked to transparency, as it involves holding government officials and institutions responsible for their actions. Effective accountability mechanisms ensure that public officials are answerable for their conduct and that there are consequences for unethical behavior (Bovens, 2007). These mechanisms can take various forms, including legal frameworks, independent oversight bodies, and participatory governance practices.

One critical aspect of accountability is the establishment of independent anti-corruption agencies that have the authority and resources to investigate and prosecute corruption cases without political interference (Johnston, 2014). These agencies should be supported by strong legal frameworks that criminalize corrupt practices and provide for the protection of whistleblowers. Additionally, accountability can be reinforced through participatory governance practices, where citizens are actively involved in decision-making processes at all levels of government, ensuring that public officials remain responsive to the needs and concerns of the people (Gaventa & McGee, 2013).

## Building Resilient Institutions

Resilient institutions are those that can withstand external shocks, adapt to changing circumstances, and continue to function effectively in the face of challenges. Building such institutions requires a proactive approach to governance that emphasizes flexibility, innovation, and inclusivity. Ethical governance plays a crucial role in this process by ensuring that institutions are built on principles of justice, equity, and the rule of law (Acemoglu & Robinson, 2012). One way to improve institutional resilience is through the adoption of adaptive governance frameworks that allow for continuous learning and improvement. These frameworks should be designed to respond to emerging social, economic, and environmental challenges by incorporating feedback mechanisms, scenario planning, and stakeholder engagement (Folke et al., 2005). Furthermore, resilient institutions must be inclusive, ensuring that all segments of society, including marginalized groups, have a voice in governance processes and access to resources and opportunities (Sen, 1999).

## Combating Corruption through Ethical Governance

Corruption is one of the most significant obstacles to ethical governance, as it undermines trust, distorts public policy, and exacerbates social inequality. To combat corruption effectively, it is essential to create systems that are resistant to corrupt practices and that promote a culture of integrity within government institutions. One effective strategy for combating corruption is the implementation of comprehensive anti-corruption policies that address both the demand and supply sides of corruption. These policies should include measures to reduce opportunities for corruption, such as streamlining administrative processes, increasing the use of technology in public service delivery, and enhancing the transparency of government contracts and procurement processes (Rose-Ackerman, 1999). Additionally, promoting a culture of integrity within public institutions is critical for preventing corruption. This can be achieved through ethics training for public officials, the establishment of clear codes of conduct, and the enforcement of strict penalties for unethical behavior (Pope, 2000).

Ethical governance is essential for creating institutional frameworks that ensure transparency, accountability, and resilience. By promoting transparency, establishing effective accountability mechanisms, building resilient institutions, and combating corruption, societies can create governance structures that are capable of adapting to changing social and economic conditions while upholding the principles of justice, equity, and the rule of law. Ultimately, ethical governance is not only about preventing negative outcomes such as corruption and inefficiency but also about fostering positive development and ensuring the long-term well- being of all citizens. Promoting ethical practices in both public and private sectors is essential for creating a fair and just society. This includes fostering a culture of integrity, encouraging responsible leadership, and implementing policies that discourage exploitative behaviors.

## The Convergence of Ideals

Despite their ideological differences, the perfect forms of capitalism and communism converge in their shared goals of fairness, innovation, and human welfare. By addressing the practical challenges of human interference and leveraging technological advancements, it is possible to move closer to a utopian vision that harmonizes the best elements of both systems. a synthesis of the ideals of capitalism and communism could offer a more balanced and pragmatic approach. By integrating the best elements of both systems, it is possible to create an economic model that promotes both individual freedom and collective welfare, while minimizing the risks of corruption and power concentration.

One potential approach is to maintain the capitalist emphasis on market competition and innovation but to regulate markets more effectively to prevent monopolies and ensure fair competition. This could involve stronger antitrust laws, more transparent regulatory processes, and the implementation of policies that promote social mobility and reduce income inequality (Stiglitz, 2012). Additionally, a focus on social entrepreneurship and corporate social responsibility could align profit motives with social goals, encouraging businesses to contribute positively to society while still pursuing financial success (Porter & Kramer, 2011).

From the communist perspective, the emphasis on equality and social welfare can be preserved through social safety nets, universal healthcare, and public education. Rather than centralizing control, these systems could be managed through decentralized, democratic processes that involve community participation and transparency (Wright, 2010). This approach would ensure that the distribution of resources is fair and equitable, while avoiding the pitfalls of authoritarianism and inefficiency.

The synthesis of capitalist and communist ideals offers a promising path toward a more just and effective economic system. By combining the strengths of both models—capitalism's dynamism and communism's commitment to equality—it is possible to create a system that better aligns with the realities of human nature and the complexities of modern society. Such a system would be better equipped to address the practical challenges of corruption, greed, and power concentration, ultimately leading to a more balanced and prosperous world.

The philosophical underpinnings of capitalism, socialism, and communism reveal a common aspiration for a just and equitable society. While historical implementations have often fallen short of these ideals, a synthesis of the best elements from each system offers a pathway toward a utopian future. By overcoming practical challenges and embracing technological innovations, we can create a society that prioritizes fairness, innovation, and the common good.

References


- Aristotle. Nicomachean Ethics.
- Aristotle. Politics.
- Autor, D. H. (2015). Why are there still so many jobs? The history and future of workplace automation. Journal of Economic Perspectives, 29(3), 3-30.
- Blomberg, Craig. (1990). Interpreting the Parables. InterVarsity Press.
- Brynjolfsson, E., & McAfee, A. (2014). The Second Machine Age: Work, Progress, and Prosperity in a Time of Brilliant Technologies. W. W. Norton & Company.
- Buckland, W.W. (1939). A Text-Book of Roman Law from Augustus to Justinian. Cambridge University Press.
- Buterin, V. (2014). A next-generation smart contract and decentralized application platform. Ethereum White Paper.
- Cato the Elder. De Agricultura.
- Cohen, Stephen F. (1974). Bukharin and the Bolshevik Revolution: A Political Biography, 1888-1938. Oxford University Press.
- Conquest, Robert. (1990).The Great Terror: A Reassessment. Oxford University Press.
- Cumings, Bruce. (2004). North Korea: Another Country. The New Press.
- Dikötter, Frank. (2010). Mao's Great Famine: The History of China's Most Devastating Catastrophe, 1958-1962. Walker & Co.
- Farber, Samuel. (2006). The Origins of the Cuban Revolution Reconsidered. University of North Carolina Press.
- Fitzpatrick, Sheila. (1994). The Russian Revolution. Oxford University Press.
- Garton Ash, Timothy. (1990). The Magic Lantern: The Revolution of '89 Witnessed in Warsaw, Budapest, Berlin, and Prague. Random House.
- Hiers, Richard H. The Historical Jesus and the Parable of the Talents (Matt 25:14-30). Perspectives in Religious Studies, 31(4), 2004, pp. 397-408.

- Kemp, Barry. (2006). Ancient Egypt: Anatomy of a Civilization. Routledge.
- Kornai, Janos. (1992). The Socialist System: The Political Economy of Communism. Princeton University Press.
- Long, A.A. (1986). Hellenistic Philosophy: Stoics, Epicureans, Sceptics. University of California Press.
- MacFarquhar, Roderick. (1997). The Politics of China: The Eras of Mao and Deng. Cambridge University Press.
- Marx, K. (1867). Das Kapital. Verlag von Otto Meisner.
- Marx, Karl, and Friedrich Engels. (1848). The Communist Manifesto.
- Nove, A. (1983). The Economics of Feasible Socialism. Allen & Unwin.
- Orwell, G. (1945). Animal Farm: A Fairy Story. Secker and Warburg.
- Piketty, Thomas. (2013). Capital in the Twenty-First Century.
- Plato. Republic.
- Russell, S., & Norvig, P. (2020). Artificial Intelligence: A Modern Approach (4th ed.). Pearson.
- Schumpeter, J. A. (2008). The Theory of Economic Development: An Inquiry into Profits, Capital, Credit, Interest, and the Business Cycle. Transaction Publishers.
- Service, Robert. Comrades! A History of World Communism. Harvard University Press, 2007.
- Smith, Adam. (1776). The Wealth of Nations.
- Snodgrass, Klyne. (2008). Stories with Intent: A Comprehensive Guide to the Parables of Jesus. Eerdmans.
- Swan, M. (2015). Blockchain: Blueprint for a New Economy. O'Reilly Media, Inc.
- Tapscott, D., & Tapscott, A. (2016). Blockchain Revolution: How the Technology Behind Bitcoin Is Changing Money, Business, and the World. Penguin.
- Weber, Max. (1905). The Protestant Ethic and the Spirit of Capitalism. Translated by Talcott Parsons, Routledge.
- Wright, A., & De Filippi, P. (2015). Decentralized blockchain technology and the rise of lex cryptographia.
- Xenophon. Oeconomicus.

## Chapter 2: Historical Case Studies on Capitalism, Socialism, and Communism

The theoretical frameworks of capitalism, socialism, and communism have been tested in various forms throughout history, providing valuable lessons about their strengths, weaknesses, and adaptability. This chapter explores four key historical case studies: the Soviet experiment, the rise of capitalism from the Industrial Revolution to the present, the implementation of socialism in Scandinavia, and the lessons learned from these historical implementations. By examining these cases, we can gain a deeper understanding of how these economic systems have evolved, succeeded, or failed, and what they can teach us about the potential for future economic models.

The Soviet Experiment: Successes and Failures

The Soviet Union's attempt to build a communist society remains one of the most significant experiments in the application of Marxist principles on a national scale. Founded in 1922, the Soviet Union sought to eliminate class distinctions and establish a state-controlled economy based on collective ownership of the means of production (Marx & Engels, 1848). The initial years of the Soviet experiment, particularly under Lenin and the early period of Stalin, were marked by rapid industrialization and efforts to create a classless society.

Successes:

- Industrialization: The Soviet Union achieved remarkable progress in industrialization, transforming from a predominantly agrarian society to a major industrial power in a few decades (Nove, 1983). The Five-Year Plans, beginning in 1928, played a crucial role in this transformation by setting ambitious targets for production and infrastructure development.
- Social Welfare: The Soviet state provided extensive social welfare programs, including universal healthcare,

education, and housing, which were aimed at ensuring that all citizens had access to basic needs (Fitzpatrick, 1999).

Failures:

- Authoritarianism and Repression: Despite its ideological commitment to equality, the Soviet state became increasingly authoritarian, particularly under Stalin. Political repression, censorship, and the purges of the 1930s contradicted the Marxist ideal of a classless and democratic society (Conquest, 1991).
- Economic Inefficiency: The centrally planned economy struggled with inefficiencies, including misallocation of resources, lack of innovation, and poor productivity, leading to stagnation and eventual economic decline in the later years (Harrison, 2002). The Soviet Union's inability to reform its economic system in the face of these challenges contributed to its collapse in 1991 (Brown, 1997).

The Rise of Capitalism: Industrial Revolution to Present

Capitalism, characterized by private ownership and market-driven economies, began to dominate Western societies during the Industrial Revolution. This period marked a profound transformation in economic and social structures, driven by technological innovation, the rise of factories, and the expansion of global trade.

Industrial Revolution:

- Economic Growth: The Industrial Revolution unleashed unprecedented economic growth, raising living standards for many and creating new opportunities for wealth creation (Mokyr, 1990). The expansion of industries such as textiles, coal, and iron laid the foundation for modern capitalist economies.
- Social Inequality: The rapid industrialization also led to significant social inequalities. The concentration of wealth and power in the hands of industrial capitalists contrasted

sharply with the poor working conditions and low wages experienced by the working class (Engels, 1845). This disparity prompted the rise of labor movements and calls for social reforms.

Modern Capitalism:

- Globalization: In the 20th and 21st centuries, capitalism has continued to evolve, with globalization playing a key role in expanding markets and integrating economies worldwide (Harvey, 2005). The rise of multinational corporations and the spread of free- market policies have led to significant economic growth, particularly in emerging economies.
- Financial Crises: Despite its successes, modern capitalism has also been marked by financial crises, such as the Great Depression of the 1930s and the Global Financial Crisis of 2008. These events have highlighted the volatility and inequality inherent in capitalist systems, leading to calls for more regulation and greater economic justice (Stiglitz, 2010).

Socialism in Scandinavia: A Hybrid Model

Scandinavian countries, particularly Sweden, Norway, and Denmark, have implemented a form of socialism that combines elements of both capitalism and socialism. This hybrid model, often referred to as the Nordic model, is characterized by a strong welfare state, high levels of taxation, and a commitment to social equality, while also embracing free markets and private ownership.

Key Features:

- Welfare State: The Nordic model is renowned for its comprehensive welfare systems, which include universal healthcare, education, and generous unemployment benefits. These programs are funded by high taxes, particularly on income and consumption, and aim to reduce inequality and provide a safety net for all citizens (Esping-Andersen, 1990).

- Economic Competitiveness: Despite the extensive welfare state, Scandinavian countries maintain competitive economies with high levels of innovation and productivity. The combination of a strong social safety net and a dynamic market economy has contributed to high standards of living and low levels of poverty (Andersen et al., 2007).

Challenges:

- Sustainability: One of the challenges facing the Nordic model is the sustainability of its welfare programs in the face of demographic changes, such as aging populations, and global economic pressures. Ensuring that the welfare state remains financially viable while maintaining economic competitiveness is a key issue for policymakers (Kangas & Palme, 2005).
- Integration and Social Cohesion: The rise of immigration in recent years has also posed challenges for social cohesion and the integration of newcomers into the welfare state. Ensuring that all members of society benefit from the system without exacerbating social tensions is a critical concern (Brochmann & Hagelund, 2012).

Lessons Learned from Historical Implementations

The historical implementations of capitalism, socialism, and communism offer valuable lessons for contemporary economic thought and policy-making. These case studies reveal the complexities and trade-offs involved in each system, as well as the potential for hybrid models that draw on the strengths of multiple approaches.

- Balance and Flexibility: One of the key lessons is the importance of balance and flexibility in economic systems. The rigidity of Soviet-style communism, with its emphasis on central planning and state control, ultimately led to its downfall. In contrast, the flexibility of capitalist systems, which allow for market-driven innovation and adaptation, has contributed to their resilience, albeit with significant social costs (Acemoglu & Robinson, 2012).

- Welfare and Inequality: The Scandinavian experience highlights the potential for combining the dynamism of capitalism with the social protections of socialism. By ensuring that economic growth is accompanied by social safety nets, it is possible to mitigate the inequalities that often arise in purely capitalist systems (Korpi & Palme, 1998).
- The Role of Governance: Effective governance is crucial in any economic system. The failures of the Soviet Union underscore the dangers of authoritarianism and the need for transparency, accountability, and democratic participation in economic decision-making (Sachs, 1995). Similarly, the financial crises in capitalist economies demonstrate the need for regulation and oversight to prevent market failures and protect the public interest (Stiglitz, 2010).

The historical case studies of the Soviet experiment, the rise of capitalism, and the Nordic model of socialism provide rich insights into the strengths and weaknesses of different economic systems. While each system has its successes and failures, the lessons learned from these experiences suggest that a hybrid approach, which combines the dynamism of capitalism with the social protections of socialism, may offer the most promising path forward. By drawing on the strengths of multiple economic ideologies and adapting to changing circumstances, societies can create more just, equitable, and sustainable economic systems.

References


- Acemoglu, D., & Robinson, J. A. (2012). Why Nations Fail: The Origins of Power, Prosperity, and Poverty. Crown Business.
- Andersen, T. M., Holmström, B., Honkapohja, S., Korkman, S., Tson, S., & Vartiainen, J. (2007). The Nordic Model: Embracing Globalization and Sharing Risks. The Research Institute of the Finnish Economy.
- Brochmann, G., & Hagelund, A. (2012). Immigration Policy and the Scandinavian Welfare State 1945-2010. Palgrave Macmillan.
- Brown, A. (1997). The Gorbachev Factor. Oxford University Press.
- Conquest, R. (1991). The Great Terror: A Reassessment. Oxford University Press.
- Engels, F. (1845). The Condition of the Working Class in England. Oxford University Press.
- Esping-Andersen, G. (1990). The Three Worlds of Welfare Capitalism. Princeton University Press.
- Fitzpatrick, S. (1999). Everyday Stalinism: Ordinary Life in Extraordinary Times: Soviet Russia in the 1930s. Oxford University Press.
- Harvey, D. (2005). A Brief History of Neoliberalism. Oxford University Press.
- Harrison, M. (2002). Coercion, Compliance, and the Collapse of the Soviet Command Economy. Economic History Review, 55(3), 397-433.
- Kangas, O., & Palme, J. (2005). Social Policy and Economic Development in the Nordic Countries. International Journal of Social Welfare, 14(4), 260-266.
- Korpi, W., & Palme, J. (1998). The Paradox of Redistribution and Strategies of Equality: Welfare State Institutions, Inequality,
- Mokyr, J. (1990). The Lever of Riches: Technological Creativity and Economic Progress. Oxford University Press.
- Nove, A. (1983). The Economics of Feasible Socialism. Allen & Unwin.

- Sachs, J. D. (1995). Russia's Struggle with Stabilization: Conceptual Issues and Evidence. World Bank Publications.
- Stiglitz, J. E. (2010). Freefall: America, Free Markets, and the Sinking of the World Economy. W. W. Norton & Company.

## Chapter 3: The Role of Technology in Shaping Economic Systems

The evolution of technology has been a driving force behind the development of economic systems throughout history. From the Industrial Revolution to the digital age, technological advancements have not only transformed production processes but have also reshaped the very foundations of economic structures. In this chapter, we look at the impact of industrialization and automation, the digital revolution with a focus on blockchain technology, the role of technology in enhancing transparency and ensuring fair contributions, and the future prospects of artificial intelligence (AI) in shaping the global economy. By examining these elements, we can better understand how technology can be harnessed to create a more equitable and effective economic system that synthesizes the strengths of capitalism and communism.

### The Impact of Industrialization and Automation

The Industrial Revolution marked a pivotal moment in the history of capitalism, fundamentally altering the modes of production and labor. The introduction of mechanized production processes, powered by steam and later electricity, enabled mass production, significantly increasing output and efficiency (Mokyr, 1990). This transformation also led to the displacement of labor, as machines began to replace human workers in various industries. This shift not only contributed to economic growth but also exacerbated social inequalities, as the benefits of industrialization were not evenly distributed (Engels, 1845).

Automation, a continuation of the industrialization trend, further intensified these dynamics. The advent of robotics and advanced manufacturing technologies in the 20th and 21st centuries has led to increased productivity and reduced costs for businesses. It has also raised concerns about job displacement and the concentration of wealth among those who control the means of production (Brynjolfsson & McAfee, 2014). As automation continues to evolve, it is crucial to consider how economic systems can adapt to ensure that the benefits of technological advancements are shared equitably across society.

## The Digital Revolution: Blockchain and Beyond

The digital revolution has dramatically transformed the global economy, ushering in a new era characterized by the rapid dissemination of information, unprecedented connectivity, and the rise of digital technologies that have fundamentally altered how businesses operate and interact with consumers. Among these technologies, blockchain stands out as one of the most transformative innovations, promising to reshape economic transactions by providing a decentralized ledger system that ensures greater transparency, security, and efficiency.

### The Transformative Potential of Blockchain Technology

Blockchain technology, at its core, is a distributed ledger that records transactions across a network of computers in a way that ensures the data is immutable and secure (Nakamoto, 2008). Each block of data is linked to the previous one, creating a chain that is nearly impossible to alter without the consensus of the entire network. This decentralization makes blockchain resistant to censorship and manipulation, providing a transparent and secure platform for economic activity (Tapscott & Tapscott, 2016).

One of the key applications of blockchain technology is in the creation of smart contracts. These are self-executing contracts where the terms of the agreement are directly written into code. Smart contracts can automatically enforce the terms of a contract once certain conditions are met, eliminating the need for intermediaries such as lawyers or brokers (Buterin, 2014). This not only reduces transaction costs but also increases trust among parties, as the contract execution is transparent and tamper-proof.

The potential applications of blockchain extend beyond simple financial transactions. For example, in supply chain management, blockchain can be used to track the provenance of goods, ensuring that products are ethically sourced and that their journey from production to the consumer is transparent (Kshetri, 2018). In the healthcare industry, blockchain can secure patient records, ensuring that data is accurate, accessible only to authorized individuals, and immutable (Agbo et al., 2019). The ability of blockchain to provide a secure, transparent, and efficient system for recording and verifying transactions makes it a powerful tool for a wide range of industries.

## The Broader Impact of Digital Technologies

Beyond blockchain, the digital revolution has introduced a range of other technologies that are reshaping industries. The Internet of Things (IoT) refers to the network of connected devices that collect and exchange data in real-time. These devices, ranging from smart thermostats to industrial sensors, enable businesses to optimize operations by providing insights into everything from energy usage to equipment maintenance (Atzori, Iera, & Morabito, 2010). IoT technology allows for the automation of processes, reducing costs and improving efficiency.

Big data analytics is another key component of the digital revolution. With the ability to process vast amounts of data, big data analytics enables businesses to gain insights into consumer behavior, market trends, and operational efficiencies. This data-driven approach allows companies to develop personalized products, tailor marketing strategies, and make informed decisions that can lead to competitive advantages (Chen, Chiang, & Storey, 2012).

The rise of digital platforms and technologies also raises significant concerns. One of the most pressing issues is data privacy. As businesses collect more data on consumers, questions arise about how this data is used and protected. The potential for surveillance and the concentration of power in the hands of a few tech giants who control vast amounts of data has led to concerns about the erosion of privacy and autonomy (Zuboff, 2019). These issues underscore the need for regulatory frameworks that protect consumers while allowing for the continued innovation and growth of digital technologies.

The digital revolution, with blockchain at the forefront, has brought about profound changes in the global economy. These technologies offer the potential for greater transparency, security, and efficiency in economic transactions, but they also present challenges related to data privacy, surveillance, and the concentration of power. As we continue to navigate this digital landscape, it is crucial to strike a balance between harnessing the benefits of these technologies and addressing the ethical and regulatory challenges they pose.

Technology and Transparency: Ensuring Fair Contributions

One of the key challenges in any economic system is ensuring that contributions are fairly recognized and rewarded. Technology can play a crucial role in enhancing transparency and accountability, helping to create a more equitable system that aligns with the ideals of both capitalism and communism.

Blockchain technology, as mentioned earlier, can provide a transparent and immutable record of transactions and contributions, making it easier to track and verify the value that individuals and organizations bring to the economy (Swan, 2015). This transparency can help prevent corruption and ensure that rewards are distributed based on merit rather than manipulation or favoritism.

Additionally, digital platforms can facilitate more direct forms of peer-to-peer exchange, bypassing traditional gatekeepers and allowing individuals to be compensated fairly for their contributions. For example, platforms like Patreon and Kickstarter enable creators to receive direct support from their audiences, fostering a more direct relationship between producers and consumers (Agrawal, Catalini, & Goldfarb, 2014). Such platforms democratize access to funding and create opportunities for individuals to contribute to the economy in ways that align with their talents and values.

## Future Prospects: AI and the Economy

Artificial intelligence (AI) represents the next frontier in the technological transformation of economic systems. AI has the potential to revolutionize industries by automating complex tasks, improving decision-making processes, and creating new products and services. AI also poses significant challenges, particularly in terms of its impact on employment, privacy, and economic inequality (Russell & Norvig, 2020).

One of the most promising applications of AI is in the field of predictive analytics, where machine learning algorithms can analyze vast amounts of data to identify patterns and make predictions. This capability can be used to optimize supply chains, personalize marketing strategies, and even predict economic trends (Agrawal, Gans, & Goldfarb, 2018). The increasing reliance on AI also raises concerns about the potential for bias in algorithms, the loss of human oversight, and the concentration of power in the hands of those who control AI technologies (O'Neil, 2016).

To harness the benefits of AI while mitigating its risks, it is essential to develop ethical guidelines and regulatory frameworks that ensure AI is used in ways that promote social welfare and economic justice (Floridi et al., 2018). By doing so, we can create an economic system that leverages AI to support productivity and innovation while ensuring that the benefits are broadly shared.

Technology has always played a crucial role in shaping economic systems, from the Industrial Revolution to the digital age. As we continue to develop and integrate new technologies such as blockchain and AI, it is essential to consider how these innovations can be harnessed to create a more equitable and effective economic system. By promoting transparency, ensuring fair contributions, and addressing the ethical challenges posed by new technologies, we can build a system that synthesizes the strengths of capitalism and communism, creating a better world and a higher quality of life for all people.

References


- Agrawal, A., Catalini, C., & Goldfarb, A. (2014). Some simple economics of crowdfunding. Innovation Policy and the Economy, 14(1), 63-97.
- Agrawal, A., Gans, J. S., & Goldfarb, A. (2018). Prediction Machines: The Simple Economics of Artificial Intelligence. Harvard Business Review Press.
- Brynjolfsson, E., & McAfee, A. (2014). The Second Machine Age: Work, Progress, and Prosperity in a Time of Brilliant Technologies. W. W. Norton & Company.
- Buterin, V. (2014). A next-generation smart contract and decentralized application platform. Ethereum White Paper.
- Evans, P. C., & Annunziata, M. (2012). Industrial Internet: Pushing the boundaries of minds and machines. General Electric.
- Floridi, L., Cowls, J., Beltrametti, M., Chatila, R., Chazerand, P., Dignum, V., ... & Vayena, E. (2018). AI4People—an ethical framework for a good AI society: Opportunities, risks, principles, and recommendations. Minds and Machines, 28(4), 689-707.
- Mokyr, J. (1990). The Lever of Riches: Technological Creativity and Economic Progress. Oxford University Press.
- O'Neil, C. (2016). Weapons of Math Destruction: How Big Data Increases Inequality and Threatens Democracy. Crown Publishing Group.
- Russell, S., & Norvig, P. (2020). Artificial Intelligence: A Modern Approach (4th ed.). Pearson.
- Swan, M. (2015). Blockchain: Blueprint for a New Economy. O'Reilly Media.
- Tapscott, D., & Tapscott, A. (2016). Blockchain Revolution: How the Technology Behind Bitcoin Is Changing Money, Business, and the World. Penguin.
- Zuboff, S. (2019). The Age of Surveillance Capitalism: The Fight for a Human Future at the New Frontier of Power. PublicAffairs.

## Chapter 4: Economic Theories and Models

Economic theories and models have evolved significantly over centuries, shaping our understanding of markets, production, distribution, and the role of government in the economy. From the foundational ideas of classical economics to the more recent developments in contemporary economic thought, these theories provide different lenses through which to analyze and address economic challenges.

### Classical and Neoclassical Economics

Classical economics, often associated with Adam Smith and David Ricardo, is grounded in the idea of free markets and the notion that individuals acting in their self-interest contribute to the complete economic good. Smith's concept of the invisible hand suggests that when individuals seek to maximize their own utility, they inadvertently contribute to societal welfare (Smith, 1776). Classical economics emphasizes the importance of competition, the division of labor, and the accumulation of capital as drivers of economic growth.

Neoclassical economics builds on the classical framework by introducing more rigorous mathematical modeling and a focus on marginalism—the analysis of incremental changes in economic variables. The neoclassical school, which includes economists such as Alfred Marshall and Léon Walras, assumes that individuals are rational actors who seek to maximize utility and firms seek to maximize profits (Marshall, 1890; Walras, 1874). This approach emphasizes the role of supply and demand in determining prices and resource allocation in markets.

Both classical and neoclassical economics have been criticized for their assumptions of rational behavior and perfect competition, which often do not hold true in real-world markets. These models also tend to overlook issues such as income inequality, market failures, and the role of government or special interest intervention (Stiglitz, 1991).

## Marxist Economic Theory

Marxist economic theory, developed by Karl Marx and Friedrich Engels, presents a stark contrast to classical and neoclassical economics. Marxism focuses on the dynamics of capitalism, particularly the conflicts between different social classes—primarily the bourgeoisie (capital owners) and the proletariat (workers). Marx argued that capitalism is inherently exploitative, as it relies on the extraction of surplus value from labor, leading to the accumulation of wealth in the hands of a few and the impoverishment of the working class (Marx, 1867).

Marxist theory predicts that the contradictions within capitalism, such as the concentration of wealth and periodic economic crises, would eventually lead to its downfall and the rise of socialism. While Marx's predictions have not fully materialized in the manner he envisioned, his critique of capitalism has influenced various movements and policies aimed at addressing social and economic inequalities (Harvey, 2010).

Marxist economics also introduces the concept of historical materialism, which posits that economic systems evolve through stages based on the development of productive forces and the relations of production. According to this view, capitalism will eventually give way to socialism as the working class becomes more organized and demands a fairer distribution of resources (Marx & Engels, 1848).

## Contemporary Economic Thought

Contemporary economic thought encompasses a wide range of schools and approaches, reflecting the complexity and diversity of modern economies. Among these are Keynesian economics, which emphasizes the role of government intervention in stabilizing the economy, particularly during periods of recession. John Maynard Keynes argued that aggregate demand— the total demand for goods and services in an economy—drives economic growth and employment. He advocated for fiscal policies, such as government spending and tax adjustments, to manage economic cycles and prevent depressions (Keynes, 1936).

Another important contemporary approach is behavioral economics, which challenges the neoclassical assumption of rationality by incorporating insights from psychology. Behavioral economists, such as Daniel Kahneman and Richard Thaler, have shown that individuals often make decisions that deviate from the rational actor model due to biases, heuristics, and other cognitive limitations (Kahneman, 2011; Thaler, 2015). This field has significant implications for public policy, marketing, and finance.

In addition to these schools, contemporary economic thought includes environmental economics, which addresses the impact of economic activity on the environment and the need for sustainable development. Economists like Nicholas Stern have argued for the incorporation of environmental costs into economic decision-making through mechanisms such as carbon pricing (Stern, 2006). This approach highlights the importance of balancing economic growth with environmental stewardship to ensure long-term prosperity.

Integrating Economic Theories for a New Model

Given the limitations and insights of the various economic theories discussed, there is a growing need to integrate these perspectives into a new economic model that addresses the challenges of the 21st century. Such a model would combine the efficiency of markets emphasized by classical and neoclassical economics with the equity concerns raised by Marxist theory and the insights into human behavior provided by behavioral economics.

One possible approach is to develop a mixed economy that leverages the strengths of both markets and government intervention. This model would allow for the allocation of resources through market mechanisms while ensuring that essential goods and services, such as healthcare and education, are accessible to all through public provision. It would also incorporate environmental considerations, recognizing that long-term economic growth depends on the sustainable use of natural resources.

Furthermore, the new model would embrace technological innovation as a driver of economic growth while addressing the potential disruptions caused by automation and digitalization. By integrating insights from various economic theories, this model would aim to create a more just, sustainable, and resilient economy that can adapt to the changing needs of society.

The evolution of economic thought has provided a vast understanding of theories and models, each offering valuable insights into how economies function and how they can be improved. By synthesizing the key ideas from classical, neoclassical, Marxist, and contemporary economic theories, we can develop a new economic model that addresses the challenges of inequality, sustainability, and technological change. This integrated approach holds the potential to create a more inclusive and prosperous future for all.

References


- Harvey, D. (2010). The Enigma of Capital: And the Crises of Capitalism. Oxford University Press.
- Kahneman, D. (2011). Thinking, Fast and Slow. Farrar, Straus and Giroux.
- Keynes, J. M. (1936). The General Theory of Employment, Interest, and Money. Palgrave Macmillan.
- Marshall, A. (1890). Principles of Economics. Macmillan.
- Marx, K. (1867). Das Kapital. Verlag von Otto Meisner.
- Marx, K., & Engels, F. (1848). The Communist Manifesto. Penguin Classics.
- Smith, A. (1776). An Inquiry into the Nature and Causes of the Wealth of Nations. W. Strahan and T. Cadell.
- Stern, N. (2006). The Stern Review: The Economics of Climate Change. Cambridge University Press.
- Stiglitz, J. E. (1991). The invisible hand and modern welfare economics. NBER Working Paper No. 3641.
- Thaler, R. H. (2015). Misbehaving: The Making of Behavioral Economics. W. W. Norton & Company.
- Walras, L. (1874). Elements of Pure Economics.

## Chapter 5: The Concept of a Contribution-Based System

The idea of a contribution-based economic system has emerged as a compelling alternative to traditional capitalist and socialist models. In a contribution-based system, economic rewards are distributed according to the value that individuals and organizations contribute to society, rather than their ownership of capital or adherence to state planning.

### Defining Contribution-Based Economics

Contribution-based economics is a framework where the distribution of resources and rewards is directly tied to the contributions made by individuals and organizations to the common good. Unlike capitalism, where rewards are largely based on market success and ownership of assets, or socialism, where distribution is typically managed by the state, a contribution-based system seeks to quantify and compensate individuals based on their actual input into society's well-being (Benkler, 2006).

This model emphasizes the value of diverse contributions, including those that are often undervalued in traditional economic systems, such as child caregiving, community service, environmental stewardship, and creative work. By aligning economic incentives with socially beneficial activities, a contribution-based system aims to foster a more equitable and sustainable economy (Bowles & Gintis, 2011).

### Mechanisms for Measuring Contributions

One of the critical tasks in a contribution-based system is developing reliable and fair mechanisms for measuring contributions. Traditional economic systems often rely on market prices or state assessments to determine value, but these approaches can overlook non- monetary contributions or distort the true value of work due to externalities and market failures (Stiglitz, Sen, & Fitoussi, 2009).

Several methods have been proposed for measuring contributions in a more comprehensive way:

- Social Impact Metrics: These involve evaluating the social, environmental, and economic impact of activities. For example, the Social Return on Investment (SROI) framework assigns a monetary value to social outcomes, allowing for a broader assessment of value creation (Nicholls, Lawlor, Neitzert, & Goodspeed, 2009).
- Collaborative Rating Systems: Peer-to-peer rating systems, similar to those used in online platforms like eBay or Airbnb, can be adapted to assess the contributions of individuals and organizations. These systems rely on the collective judgment of the community to evaluate the quality and impact of contributions (Benkler, 2017).
- Data-Driven Analytics: With the advent of big data and AI, it is possible to develop algorithms that track and analyze contributions in real-time, providing a dynamic and ongoing assessment of value creation (Brynjolfsson & McAfee, 2014). These analytics can be used to allocate rewards in a way that reflects the true value of contributions to society.

Digital Contracts and Blockchain: Ensuring Fairness

Blockchain technology and digital contracts play a crucial role in ensuring fairness and transparency in a contribution-based economic system. Blockchain's decentralized nature allows for the creation of immutable records of transactions and contributions, which can be verified by all participants in the network (Tapscott & Tapscott, 2016). This transparency reduces the potential for fraud and manipulation, ensuring that rewards are distributed based on actual contributions.

Smart contracts, which are self-executing contracts with the terms directly written into code, can automate the process of rewarding contributions. These contracts can be programmed to release payments or other rewards when certain conditions are met, such as the completion of a project or the achievement of specific outcomes (Buterin, 2014). This automation not only reduces administrative costs but also ensures that contributors are compensated fairly and promptly.

Blockchain's ability to provide a transparent and secure record of contributions also supports the development of new economic models, such as decentralized autonomous organizations (DAOs), where decision-making and resource allocation are managed collectively by stakeholders through digital contracts (Wright & De Filippi, 2015). These models align with the principles of a contribution-based economy by promoting collective ownership and participation in economic governance.

Case Studies: Successful Implementation of Contribution Models

Several real-world examples illustrate the potential of contribution-based models to create more equitable and sustainable economies:

- Fair Trade Certification: Fair Trade is a global movement that seeks to ensure that producers in developing countries are paid fair prices for their goods and are recognized for their contributions to sustainable development. By certifying products that meet social, environmental, and economic standards, Fair Trade provides a model for rewarding contributions based on their impact on global welfare (Raynolds, Murray, & Wilkinson, 2007).
- Open-Source Software Development: The open-source software movement is an example of a contribution-based model in the digital economy. Developers contribute code, documentation, and other resources to open-source projects, and their contributions are often recognized through community endorsements, reputation systems, and, in some cases, financial rewards (Weber, 2004). This model demonstrates how collaborative efforts can create valuable public goods while rewarding contributors in non-traditional ways.
- Cooperative Businesses: Cooperatives are businesses owned and run by their members, who share the profits and make decisions collectively. This model aligns with

the principles of contribution-based economics by ensuring that those who contribute to the success of the business are also the ones who benefit from it. Examples include cooperative banks, grocery stores, and worker-owned enterprises (Birchall, 2011).

A contribution-based economic system offers a promising alternative to traditional models by aligning rewards with the actual value that individuals and organizations bring to society. By leveraging mechanisms such as social impact metrics, collaborative rating systems, and blockchain technology, it is possible to create a fairer and more transparent economy. The successful implementation of contribution models in various sectors demonstrates the potential of this approach to foster a more equitable and sustainable world.

Challenges in Implementing Contribution-Based Systems

1. Measuring and Valuing Contributions

One of the most critical challenges in implementing contribution-based systems is accurately measuring and valuing contributions. Traditional economic models often rely on market prices or state-determined metrics, which may not fully capture the value of non-market activities such as caregiving, environmental stewardship, or creative work (Stiglitz, Sen, & Fitoussi, 2009). The subjective nature of value and the difficulty in quantifying intangible contributions complicate the establishment of a fair and transparent system for rewarding contributions.

The diversity of contributions—ranging from intellectual and creative inputs to labor and social capital—requires a multi-faceted approach to measurement that can account for different forms of value creation (Benkler, 2006). The development of reliable metrics that reflect the true societal impact of various contributions is essential but remains a significant challenge.

2. Technological and Infrastructural Barriers

While digital technologies such as blockchain and AI offer promising tools for implementing contribution-based systems, they also present technological and infrastructural challenges. For example, blockchain's scalability and energy consumption issues need to be addressed to make it a viable solution for large-scale contribution tracking (Swan, 2015). Additionally, the digital divide—disparities in access to technology and the internet—can exacerbate inequalities, preventing some individuals and communities from fully participating in and benefiting from these systems (Norris, 2001).

The integration of advanced technologies into existing economic infrastructures also requires significant investment and coordination across multiple sectors, including government, private industry, and civil society. Overcoming these barriers is crucial to ensuring that contribution- based systems are inclusive and accessible to all.

3. Governance and Regulatory Challenges

Implementing a contribution-based system involves rethinking traditional governance structures and developing new regulatory frameworks. Ensuring that these systems are fair, transparent, and resistant to corruption requires oversight mechanisms and clear legal guidelines (Wright & De Filippi, 2015). The decentralized nature of contribution-based systems, particularly those built on blockchain technology, complicates the establishment of centralized regulatory authorities.

There is also the challenge of aligning the interests of various stakeholders—governments, businesses, and individuals—in a way that supports the widespread adoption and sustainability of contribution-based systems. Developing governance models that balance decentralized decision-making with effective regulation is essential to the success of these systems (Tapscott & Tapscott, 2016).

## Opportunities in Contribution-Based Systems

### 1. Promoting Equity and Inclusion

One of the most significant opportunities presented by contribution-based systems is the potential to promote greater equity and inclusion in the economy. By recognizing and rewarding a broader range of contributions, these systems can help address the inequalities that are often perpetuated by traditional economic models. For example, activities that are typically undervalued or uncompensated—such as caregiving, community organizing, and environmental conservation—can be more appropriately recognized and rewarded, leading to a more equitable distribution of resources (Folbre, 2001).

Contribution-based systems also have the potential to empower marginalized communities by providing them with new opportunities to participate in the economy. Digital platforms and decentralized technologies can reduce barriers to entry, enabling individuals and groups to contribute in ways that were previously inaccessible (Benkler, 2017). This inclusivity can lead to more diverse and resilient economic systems.

### 2. Enhancing Sustainability

Contribution-based systems offer a framework for promoting sustainability by aligning economic incentives with environmental and social goals. By rewarding contributions that support sustainable practices—such as reducing carbon emissions, conserving natural resources, and promoting social well-being—these systems can drive more sustainable economic behaviors (Jackson, 2009). This alignment of incentives is crucial for addressing global challenges such as climate change, resource depletion, and social inequality.

Additionally, the use of digital technologies in contribution-based systems can improve transparency and accountability, making it easier to track the environmental and social impacts of economic activities. This transparency can help consumers make more informed choices and encourage businesses to adopt more sustainable practices (Kshetri, 2018).

3. Fostering Innovation

Contribution-based systems can also foster innovation by creating new incentives for creativity and collaboration. By recognizing and rewarding contributions to open-source projects, research, and other collaborative efforts, these systems can support the development of new ideas and technologies that benefit society as a whole (Weber, 2004). The decentralized nature of contribution-based systems encourages experimentation and the sharing of knowledge, which can lead to breakthroughs in various fields.

The use of smart contracts and blockchain technology can streamline the innovation process by automating the distribution of rewards and reducing transaction costs. This efficiency can accelerate the development and dissemination of new ideas, making it easier for innovators to bring their contributions to market (Buterin, 2014).

Strategies for Overcoming Challenges

1. Developing Comprehensive Metrics for Contributions

To address the challenge of measuring and valuing contributions, it is essential to develop comprehensive and multi-dimensional metrics that reflect the diverse ways in which individuals and organizations create value. This may involve combining quantitative measures, such as social impact metrics and data-driven analytics, with qualitative assessments, such as peer reviews and community ratings (Nicholls et al., 2009). Engaging stakeholders in the development of these metrics can help ensure that they are fair, transparent, and aligned with societal values.

2. Investing in Technology and Infrastructure

Overcoming technological and infrastructural barriers requires significant investment in digital infrastructure, including expanding access to high-speed internet and digital literacy programs. Governments, businesses, and international organizations must collaborate to ensure that the benefits of contribution-based systems are accessible to all, regardless of geographic location or socioeconomic status (Norris, 2001).

Furthermore, addressing the scalability and energy efficiency of blockchain and other digital technologies is crucial for their widespread adoption. Ongoing research and development in these areas can help overcome technical challenges and make these technologies more sustainable (Swan, 2015).

3. Establishing Effective Governance and Regulatory Frameworks

Developing effective governance and regulatory frameworks is essential for ensuring that contribution-based systems are fair, transparent, and resistant to corruption. This may involve creating new institutions or adapting existing ones to oversee the implementation and operation of these systems. Additionally, fostering collaboration between governments, businesses, and civil society can help align interests and ensure that these systems are designed and operated in the public interest (Wright & De Filippi, 2015).

Establishing clear legal guidelines and ethical standards for the use of digital technologies in contribution-based systems is also critical. This includes addressing issues such as data privacy, security, and the ethical use of AI and blockchain (Floridi et al., 2018). By developing effective regulatory framework, it is possible to create a stable and trustworthy environment for contribution-based systems to thrive.

Implementing contribution-based economic systems presents both challenges and opportunities. While there are significant hurdles to overcome—such as measuring contributions, addressing technological barriers, and establishing effective governance—there are also remarkable opportunities to promote equity, sustainability, and innovation. By developing comprehensive metrics, investing in technology and infrastructure, and establishing strong governance frameworks, it is possible to create a contribution-based system that fosters a more just, inclusive, and sustainable economy.

References


- Benkler, Y. (2006). The Wealth of Networks: How Social Production Transforms Markets and Freedom. Yale University Press.
- Benkler, Y. (2017). Peer production, the commons, and the future of the firm. Strategic Organization, 15(2), 264-274.
- Birchall, J. (2011). People-Centred Businesses: Co-operatives, Mutuals and the Idea of Membership. Palgrave Macmillan.
- Bowles, S., & Gintis, H. (2011). A Cooperative Species: Human Reciprocity and Its Evolution. Princeton University Press.
- Brynjolfsson, E., & McAfee, A. (2014). The Second Machine Age: Work, Progress, and Prosperity in a Time of Brilliant Technologies. W. W. Norton & Company.
- Buterin, V. (2014). A next-generation smart contract and decentralized application platform. Ethereum White Paper.
- Folbre, N. (2001). The Invisible Heart: Economics and Family Values. The New Press.
- Floridi, L., Cowls, J., Beltrametti, M., Chatila, R., Chazerand, P., Dignum, V., ... & Vayena, E. (2018). AI4People—an ethical framework for a good AI society: Opportunities, risks, principles, and recommendations. Minds and Machines, 28(4), 689-707.
- Jackson, T. (2009). Prosperity without Growth: Economics for a Finite Planet. Earthscan.
- Kshetri, N. (2018). Blockchain's roles in meeting key supply chain management objectives. International Journal of Information Management, 39, 80-89.
- Nicholls, J., Lawlor, E., Neitzert, E., & Goodspeed, T. (2009). A guide to Social Return on Investment. The SROI Network.

- Norris, P. (2001). Digital Divide: Civic Engagement, Information Poverty, and the Internet Worldwide. Cambridge University Press.
- Raynolds, L. T., Murray, D., & Wilkinson, J. (2007). Fair Trade: The Challenges of Transforming Globalization. Routledge.
- Stiglitz, J. E., Sen, A., & Fitoussi, J. P. (2009). Report by the Commission on the Measurement of Economic Performance and Social Progress. Commission on the Measurement of Economic Performance and Social Progress.
- Swan, M. (2015). Blockchain: Blueprint for a New Economy. O'Reilly Media.
- Tapscott, D., & Tapscott, A. (2016). Blockchain Revolution: How the Technology Behind Bitcoin Is Changing Money, Business, and the World. Penguin.
- Weber, S. (2004). The Success of Open Source. Harvard University Press.
- Wright, A., & De Filippi, P. (2015). Decentralized blockchain technology and the rise of lex cryptographia.

## Chapter 6: Overcoming Human Interference

Human interference in economic systems, manifesting as corruption, greed, and exploitation; has long been a significant challenge to creating equitable and effective economies. These issues undermine trust in institutions, exacerbate inequality, and hinder the fair distribution of resources. To overcome these challenges, it is essential to develop effective governance and regulatory frameworks, mitigate corruption, promote ethical practices, and create systems that are resistant to exploitation.

### The Role of Governance and Regulation

Effective governance and regulation are foundational to overcoming human interference in economic systems. Governance involves the structures and processes by which decisions are made and implemented, while regulation refers to the rules and standards that govern behavior within these systems (North, 1990). Together, they create the framework within which economic activities occur, ensuring that they align with broader societal goals.

Strong governance and regulatory frameworks are essential for maintaining transparency, accountability, and fairness in economic systems. They help prevent the concentration of power, which can lead to corruption and exploitation, by ensuring that decision-making processes are inclusive and representative of all stakeholders (Rodrik, 2007). Additionally, these frameworks establish the legal and ethical standards that guide economic behavior, deterring misconduct and promoting responsible practices (Acemoglu & Robinson, 2012).

Governance structures should also be adaptable, allowing for the continuous refinement of regulations to address emerging challenges and changing circumstances. This flexibility is particularly important in a rapidly evolving economic landscape, where new technologies and globalization present both opportunities and risks (Florini, 2011). By fostering a dynamic and responsive governance system, societies can better navigate the complexities of modern economies while safeguarding against human interference.

## Mitigating Corruption and Greed

Corruption and greed are among the most pernicious forms of human interference in economic systems. They distort markets, erode trust in institutions, and contribute to inequality by allowing a select few to manipulate the system for personal gain. To mitigate these issues, it is crucial to implement strategies that improve transparency, strengthen accountability, and reduce opportunities for corrupt practices.

One effective approach is the establishment of independent anti-corruption agencies that have the authority and resources to investigate and prosecute corruption cases (Johnston, 2014). These agencies should operate free from political interference and be empowered to hold even the most powerful individuals and organizations accountable. Additionally, transparency initiatives, such as open data platforms and public access to government records, can help expose corrupt practices and empower citizens to demand accountability (Meijer, 2015).

Another important strategy is the promotion of a culture of integrity within both public and private sectors. This can be achieved through ethics training, the establishment of clear codes of conduct, and the enforcement of strict penalties for unethical behavior (Pope, 2000). By fostering a culture that values honesty, fairness, and responsibility, societies can reduce the influence of greed and promote more ethical economic practices.

## Promoting Ethical Practices in Economics

Ethical practices in economics involve adhering to principles of fairness, justice, and respect for human dignity in all economic activities. Promoting ethical practices is essential for creating an economy that serves the common good and protects the rights and well-being of all participants.

Education and awareness are key to promoting ethical practices. By integrating ethics into the curriculum of economics and business education, future leaders can be better prepared to make decisions that align with ethical standards (Sen, 1999). Additionally, public awareness campaigns can help inform consumers, investors, and workers about the importance of ethical practices, encouraging them to support businesses and policies that prioritize ethics.

Corporate social responsibility (CSR) is another important avenue for promoting ethical practices. CSR involves businesses voluntarily committing to ethical standards in areas such as labor practices, environmental sustainability, and community engagement (Porter & Kramer, 2011). By embracing CSR, businesses can contribute to a more ethical economy while also enhancing their reputation and building trust with stakeholders.

Regulatory frameworks should include provisions that encourage or mandate ethical practices, such as requirements for environmental stewardship, fair labor standards, and corporate transparency. These regulations can help level the playing field, ensuring that businesses that prioritize ethics are not at a competitive disadvantage (Stiglitz, 2012).

Creating Systems Resistant to Exploitation

To create an economic system resistant to exploitation, it is necessary to design mechanisms that prevent the concentration of power and ensure that economic benefits are broadly distributed. This involves both structural reforms and the use of technology to safeguard against exploitation.

Decentralization is one structural approach that can help reduce the potential for exploitation. By distributing decision-making authority across multiple levels of government and involving a diverse range of stakeholders, decentralization can limit the ability of any single entity to dominate the system (Ostrom, 1990). This approach also encourages greater participation and accountability, as decisions are made closer to the affected communities.

In addition to structural reforms, technology can play a critical role in creating systems resistant to exploitation. Blockchain technology, for example, offers a decentralized and transparent way to record transactions, reducing the opportunities for fraud and manipulation (Tapscott & Tapscott, 2016). Similarly, AI and big data analytics can be used to monitor economic activities in real-time, identifying and addressing potential exploitation before it escalates (Brynjolfsson & McAfee, 2014).

Finally, legal and regulatory frameworks must be continuously updated to address new forms of exploitation that may arise with technological advancements. This includes protecting against digital exploitation, such as data breaches and surveillance capitalism, and ensuring that emerging technologies are used in ways that benefit society as a whole (Zuboff, 2019).

Overcoming human interference in economic systems requires a multivariate approach that includes strong governance and regulation, strategies to mitigate corruption and greed, the promotion of ethical practices, and the creation of systems resistant to exploitation. By addressing these challenges, societies can build economic systems that are fairer, more transparent, and more resilient, ultimately contributing to a more just and sustainable world.

References


- Acemoglu, D., & Robinson, J. A. (2012). Why Nations Fail: The Origins of Power, Prosperity, and Poverty. Crown Business.
- Brynjolfsson, E., & McAfee, A. (2014). The Second Machine Age: Work, Progress, and Prosperity in a Time of Brilliant Technologies. W. W. Norton & Company.
- Florini, A. (2011). The Right to Know: Transparency for an Open World. Columbia University Press.
- Johnston, M. (2014). Corruption, Contention, and Reform: The Power of Deep Democratization. Cambridge University Press.

- Meijer, A. (2015). Transparency. Public Administration Review, 75(4), 472-482.
- North, D. C. (1990). Institutions, Institutional Change and Economic Performance. Cambridge University Press.
- Ostrom, E. (1990). Governing the Commons: The Evolution of Institutions for Collective Action. Cambridge University Press.
- Pope, J. (2000). Confronting Corruption: The Elements of a National Integrity System. Transparency International.
- Porter, M. E., & Kramer, M. R. (2011). Creating shared value: How to reinvent capitalism—and unleash a wave of innovation and growth. Harvard Business Review, 89(1/2), 62-77.
- Rodrik, D. (2007). One Economics, Many Recipes: Globalization, Institutions, and Economic Growth. Princeton University Press.
- Sen, A. (1999). Development as Freedom. Oxford University Press.
- Stiglitz, J. E. (2012). The Price of Inequality: How Today's Divided Society Endangers Our Future. W. W. Norton & Company.
- Tapscott, D., & Tapscott, A. (2016). Blockchain Revolution: How the Technology Behind Bitcoin Is Changing Money, Business, and the World. Penguin.
- Zuboff, S. (2019). The Age of Surveillance Capitalism: The Fight for a Human Future at the New Frontier of Power. PublicAffairs.

## Chapter 7: Synthesizing Communism and Capitalism

Communism and capitalism represent two of the most influential and contrasting economic ideologies in modern history. While capitalism emphasizes individual freedom, private ownership, and market-driven economies, communism focuses on collective ownership, equality, and state control of resources. These ideologies have often been seen as incompatible, but the growing complexity of global challenges necessitates a re-examination of how elements from both systems can be synthesized to create a more balanced and equitable economic model.

The Ideals of Communism and Capitalism

Capitalism is rooted in the ideals of individualism, private property, and free markets. The theory posits that when individuals pursue their self-interest within a competitive marketplace, resources are allocated efficiently, leading to innovation, economic growth, and general societal prosperity (Smith, 1776). The capitalist model advocates minimal state intervention, with the belief that the invisible hand of the market is the best mechanism for coordinating economic activity (Hayek, 1944).

Communism, on the other hand, is based on the ideals of equality, collective ownership, and the elimination of class distinctions. Marxist theory argues that capitalism inherently leads to exploitation and inequality, as the means of production are controlled by a small elite who extract surplus value from the labor of the working class (Marx, 1867). Communism seeks to abolish private property, redistribute wealth, and establish a classless society where resources are shared according to need rather than profit (Engels, 1878).

These contrasting ideals have shaped the political and economic landscapes of the 20th and 21st centuries. Conversely, both systems have faced significant challenges in practice. Capitalism has been criticized for leading to income inequality, environmental degradation, and economic instability, while communist experiments have often resulted in authoritarianism, economic inefficiency, and a lack of individual freedoms (Fukuyama, 1992; Harvey, 2010).

## Harmonizing Collective and Individual Interests

To create a more balanced economic system, it is essential to find ways to harmonize the collective interests emphasized by communism with the individual freedoms central to capitalism. This harmonization can be achieved by recognizing that both collective and individual interests are essential for the well-being of society.

Collective Interests: Communism's emphasis on equality and collective ownership can be incorporated into a synthesized model through the development of social safety nets, universal access to education and healthcare, and mechanisms for wealth redistribution. These measures ensure that all members of society have access to basic needs and opportunities, thereby reducing inequality and fostering social cohesion (Rawls, 1971).

Individual Interests: Capitalism's focus on individual freedom and innovation can be preserved by maintaining a market-based economy that rewards creativity, entrepreneurship, and risk-taking. This market system can be regulated to prevent monopolies, ensure fair competition, and protect the environment. By balancing these individual interests with collective welfare, it is possible to create an economy that is both dynamic and equitable (Sen, 1999).

The key to harmonizing these interests lies in developing institutions and policies that align individual incentives with the common good. For example, tax policies can be designed to encourage charitable giving and social investment, while businesses can be incentivized to adopt sustainable practices that benefit society as a whole (Porter & Kramer, 2011).

Practical Steps Toward Synthesis

Synthesizing the ideals of communism and capitalism requires practical steps that involve both policy innovations and institutional reforms. Some of these steps include:

1. Progressive Taxation and Wealth Redistribution: Implementing progressive tax policies that ensure the wealthy contribute a fair share to public goods can help reduce income inequality without stifling economic growth. The revenue generated can be used to fund universal healthcare, education, and other social programs (Piketty, 2014).
2. Public-Private Partnerships: Encouraging collaboration between the public and private sectors can combine the efficiency of markets with the equity goals of state intervention. Public-private partnerships can be particularly effective in addressing large-scale challenges such as infrastructure development, climate change, and social welfare (Kuttner, 2019).
3. Corporate Social Responsibility (CSR) and Stakeholder Capitalism: Promoting CSR and shifting towards stakeholder capitalism, where businesses consider the interests of all stakeholders (including employees, customers, and communities) rather than just shareholders, can align corporate behavior with social and environmental goals (Freeman, 1984).
4. Participatory Governance: Developing governance structures that involve citizens in decision-making processes can ensure that both individual and collective interests are represented. This can include mechanisms for direct democracy, participatory budgeting, and community-led development initiatives (Ostrom, 1990).
5. Sustainable Development Goals (SDGs): Aligning economic policies with the United Nations' SDGs can provide a framework for integrating the social equity goals of communism with the economic dynamism of capitalism. The SDGs emphasize inclusive economic growth, environmental sustainability, and social justice,

which are essential components of a synthesized economic model (United Nations, 2015).

## Vision of a Converged Economic System

The ultimate vision of a synthesized economic system is one that integrates the strengths of both communism and capitalism while mitigating their respective weaknesses. Such a system would prioritize human well-being, social equity, and environmental sustainability, while also fostering innovation, economic growth, and individual freedom.

Key Features of the Converged System:

- Inclusive Markets: Markets would remain the primary mechanism for resource allocation, but they would be regulated to ensure fairness, prevent exploitation, and protect the environment. Economic policies would be designed to promote competition, innovation, and entrepreneurship, while also ensuring that the benefits of economic growth are broadly shared.
- Universal Basic Services: The state would guarantee access to essential services such as healthcare, education, and housing, ensuring that all citizens have the basic resources they need to live fulfilling lives. These services would be funded through progressive taxation and wealth redistribution.
- Democratic Governance: Governance structures would be designed to involve citizens in decision-making processes, ensuring that economic policies reflect the needs and values of the entire society. This would include mechanisms for participatory governance, transparency, and accountability.
- Sustainable Development: The economy would be aligned with sustainable development goals, prioritizing long-term environmental sustainability and social justice over short-term profit maximization. Businesses would be encouraged to adopt sustainable practices, and the state would invest in green technologies and infrastructure.

This converged economic system represents a new paradigm that moves beyond the dichotomy of communism and capitalism. By synthesizing the best elements of both ideologies, it is possible to create a more just, equitable, and sustainable economy that meets the needs of all people.

Synthesizing communism and capitalism offers a path toward a more balanced and effective economic system. By harmonizing collective and individual interests, implementing practical steps toward synthesis, and envisioning a converged economic model, we can create an economy that promotes both social equity and economic dynamism. This integrated approach has the potential to address the challenges of the 21st century and create a better world for future generations.

References


- Acemoglu, D., & Robinson, J. A. (2012). Why Nations Fail: The Origins of Power, Prosperity, and Poverty. Crown Business.
- Engels, F. (1878). Anti-Dühring: Herr Eugen Dühring's Revolution in Science. Marxist Library.
- Freeman, R. E. (1984). Strategic Management: A Stakeholder Approach. Pitman Publishing.
- Fukuyama, F. (1992). The End of History and the Last Man. Free Press.
- Harvey, D. (2010). The Enigma of Capital: And the Crises of Capitalism. Oxford University Press.
- Hayek, F. A. (1944). The Road to Serfdom. University of Chicago Press.
- Kuttner, R. (2019). Can Democracy Survive Global Capitalism? W. W. Norton & Company.
- Marx, K. (1867). Das Kapital. Verlag von Otto Meisner.
- Ostrom, E. (1990). Governing the Commons: The Evolution of Institutions for Collective Action. Cambridge University Press.
- Piketty, T. (2014). Capital in the Twenty-First Century. Harvard University Press.
- Porter, M. E., & Kramer, M. R. (2011). Creating shared value: How to reinvent capitalism—and unleash a wave of innovation and growth. Harvard Business Review, 89(1/2), 62-77.
- Rawls, J. (1971). A Theory of Justice. Harvard University Press.
- Sen, A. (1999). Development as Freedom. Oxford University Press.
- Smith, A. (1776). An Inquiry into the Nature and Causes of the Wealth of Nations. W. Strahan and T. Cadell.
- United Nations. (2015). Transforming Our World: The 2030 Agenda for Sustainable Development. United Nations.

## Chapter 8: The Path to Utopia

The concept of utopia has captivated human imagination for centuries, representing the ideal of a perfect society where justice, equality, and happiness prevail. While the idea of a utopian society remains a powerful aspiration, translating this vision into reality presents significant theoretical and practical challenges. Researchers, scholars, politicians, individuals and philosophers alike must look at the theoretical foundations of utopian societies, the practical obstacles to achieving utopia, the role of global cooperation and community in this endeavor and conclude whether utopia is truly achievable.

### Theoretical Foundations of Utopian Societies

The idea of utopia has its roots in classical philosophy and literature. The term utopia was coined by Sir Thomas More in his 1516 book Utopia, which depicted an ideal society on an imaginary island. More's utopia was characterized by communal ownership, equality, and rational governance—an ideal that contrasted sharply with the social and political realities of his time (More, 1516). Utopian thought has since evolved, influencing various social, political, and economic theories.

Marxism: Karl Marx's vision of a classless society, where the means of production are communally owned and wealth is distributed according to need, represents a form of utopian thinking. Marx believed that the contradictions of capitalism would eventually lead to its collapse and the emergence of a socialist utopia, where exploitation and inequality would be eliminated (Marx, 1867). Marx's utopia was not a static end-state but a dynamic process of continual improvement and social progress.

Anarchism: Anarchist theorists such as Peter Kropotkin and Mikhail Bakunin envisioned a utopian society based on voluntary cooperation, mutual aid, and the abolition of hierarchical structures. In contrast to Marxist theory, anarchism emphasizes decentralization and the rejection of state authority as the path to achieving a utopian society (Kropotkin, 1902; Bakunin, 1873).

Liberalism: In the liberal tradition, utopian ideals are often associated with the protection of individual rights, the rule of law, and the promotion of democratic governance. Thinkers like John Stuart Mill and Immanuel Kant envisioned societies where freedom, justice, and moral progress are achieved through the development of rational institutions and the cultivation of individual autonomy (Mill, 1859; Kant, 1795).

While these theoretical foundations provide different visions of utopia, they all share a common belief in the possibility of creating a better world through the transformation of social, political, and economic structures.

Practical Challenges and Solutions

The path to utopia is fraught with practical challenges. One of the primary obstacles is the inherent complexity of human societies, where diverse interests, values, and power dynamics often lead to conflict and inequality. Additionally, historical attempts to create utopian societies have often resulted in unintended consequences, such as authoritarianism, economic inefficiency, or social unrest (Popper, 1945).

Challenge 1: Human Nature and Social Complexity: Utopian visions often assume a level of human cooperation and altruism that may be unrealistic given the complexities of human behavior. The diversity of human interests, cultural differences, and the tendency toward self- interest can make it difficult to achieve the level of harmony and equality envisioned in utopian theories (Freud, 1930).

Solution: Addressing this challenge requires a more nuanced understanding of human nature and the development of institutions that can mediate conflicts and balance competing interests. Participatory governance, social contracts, and mechanisms for conflict resolution can help create a more harmonious society without requiring individuals to completely abandon their self-interests (Rawls, 1971). Helping all individuals improve their mental, psychological, physical and spiritual ability to work in a common ecosystem is mandatory for this endeavor.

Mental health is a reality, and if the system is improved we can all work together to make the world a better place for everyone.

Challenge 2: Economic and Environmental Sustainability: Utopian societies often envision a world of abundance and ecological harmony. Achieving this vision in practice is complicated by the finite nature of resources, environmental degradation, and the challenges of managing complex economies (Ostrom, 1990).

Solution: Sustainable development practices, such as the adoption of renewable energy, circular economies, and sustainable agriculture, are essential for addressing these challenges. Additionally, technological innovation and global cooperation are crucial for ensuring that economic and environmental sustainability are integrated into the path toward utopia (Meadows et al., 1972).

Challenge 3: Political Power and Authority: The concentration of political power has been a significant barrier to the realization of utopian ideals. Historically, attempts to create utopian societies have often led to the rise of authoritarian regimes that suppress dissent and concentrate power in the hands of a few (Arendt, 1951).

Solution: Decentralization of power, democratic participation, and the establishment of checks and balances are essential for preventing the concentration of authority and ensuring that governance structures remain accountable to the people. Building strong civil society organizations and promoting transparency in governance can help create a more democratic and just society (Dahl, 1989).

The Role of Global Cooperation and Community

Global cooperation is crucial for the realization of utopian ideals in an interconnected world. Challenges such as climate change, economic inequality, and armed conflict transcend national borders and require collective action on a global scale (Held & McGrew, 2002).

Global Governance: Institutions such as the United Nations, the World Bank, and the World Health Organization play a critical role in coordinating international efforts to address global challenges. Strengthening these institutions and ensuring that they operate in a transparent and inclusive manner is essential for fostering global cooperation (Stiglitz, 2002).

Community Building: At the local level, building strong communities based on mutual aid, cooperation, and shared values is essential for creating a foundation for global solidarity. Community-led initiatives, such as cooperatives, local currencies, and participatory budgeting, can help empower individuals and create resilient networks that contribute to the broader goal of global cooperation (Ostrom, 1990).

Technology and Communication: The rise of digital technologies and global communication networks has opened new possibilities for global cooperation. Social media, online platforms, and blockchain technology can facilitate cross-border collaboration, transparency, and enable the sharing of knowledge and resources on a global scale (Castells, 2010). It is also important to address the challenges posed by digital surveillance, misinformation, and the digital divide to ensure that technology serves as a tool for empowerment rather than control (Zuboff, 2019).

Final Reflections: Is Utopia Achievable?

The question of whether utopia is achievable remains a matter of debate. While utopian visions provide a powerful impetus for social change, the complexities of human societies and the challenges of implementation suggest that a perfect society may always remain out of reach.

Still, the pursuit of utopia is valuable not because it offers a final destination, but because it inspires continuous efforts to improve the world.

Incremental Progress: Rather than focusing on the attainment of a perfect society, it may be more practical to pursue incremental progress toward utopian ideals. This approach emphasizes the importance of ongoing social, political, and economic reforms that gradually move society closer to the vision of utopia (Sen, 1999). By setting realistic goals and continuously striving for improvement, it is possible to achieve meaningful progress toward a more just and equitable world.

The Role of Ideals: Utopian ideals serve as a course for standard operating procedures, providing direction and motivation for collective efforts to create a better world. While the full realization of utopia may be unattainable, the pursuit of these ideals can lead to significant advancements in human rights, social justice, and environmental sustainability (Levitas, 2013).

The path to utopia is not a straightforward journey but a continuous process of striving for improvement. While the challenges are formidable, the pursuit of utopian ideals can inspire collective action, global cooperation, and the development of innovative solutions to the world's most pressing problems. By embracing both the theoretical foundations and the practical realities of utopian thought, we can work toward creating a world that, while not perfect, is significantly better than the one we have today.

The ideological dichotomy between capitalism and communism has dominated global economic and political discourse for over a century. Capitalism, characterized by private ownership, free markets, and profit motives, contrasts starkly with communism's focus on collective ownership, state control, and the eradication of class distinctions. While both systems have achieved significant historical successes, they have also led to considerable social, economic, and political challenges. As we move further into the 21st century, the need to synthesize these seemingly opposing ideologies has become increasingly urgent. Failure to do so could result in numerous disadvantages and existential threats to society, including economic inequality, political instability, environmental degradation, and social disintegration.

## The Problem of Economic Inequality

Economic inequality has emerged as one of the most pressing issues in contemporary society. Capitalism's emphasis on individual success and wealth accumulation has led to significant disparities in income and wealth distribution. According to Piketty (2014), the concentration of wealth in the hands of a small elite is not a temporary aberration but a structural feature of capitalism, driven by the rate of return on capital outpacing economic growth. This trend exacerbates social stratification, leading to a two-tier society where the rich continue to accumulate wealth while the poor face increasing hardships.

Communism, in its pure form, seeks to eliminate these disparities by abolishing private property and redistributing wealth. Despite efforts to end these disparities , historical struggles at implementing communism have often resulted in authoritarian regimes that suppress individual freedoms and fail to achieve the promised economic equality (Djilas, 1957). The inability to reconcile the efficiency and innovation of capitalism with the equity and social justice goals of communism has left societies vulnerable to deepening economic divides.

If society does not find a way to synthesize these ideologies, the gap between the rich and poor will likely widen, leading to increased social unrest, higher crime rates, and a breakdown of social cohesion. The persistence of extreme inequality can erode trust in institutions and fuel populist movements that exploit economic grievances, potentially destabilizing democratic governance (Stiglitz, 2012).

## Political Instability and Authoritarianism

The failure to synthesize capitalist and communist ideals also poses significant risks to political stability. Capitalism, with its emphasis on market-driven policies, can undermine the state's ability to provide essential services and maintain social welfare. This can lead to a legitimacy crisis, where the state is perceived as serving the interests of the wealthy elite rather than the broader population (Harvey, 2005). On the other hand, communism's emphasis on state control and centralized planning often leads to bureaucratic inefficiencies and a lack of political freedoms, as evidenced by the Soviet Union's collapse.

Without a synthesis that balances the strengths and weaknesses of both systems, societies may experience a resurgence of authoritarianism, where leaders exploit economic instability and social divisions to consolidate power. This could manifest in the form of illiberal democracies, where democratic institutions exist in name only, or in outright autocracies that suppress dissent and curtail individual freedoms (Levitsky & Ziblatt, 2018). The erosion of people- centered norms and institutions can have far-reaching consequences, including the stifling of innovation, the marginalization of minority groups, and the perpetuation of systemic corruption.

Environmental Degradation

Another significant threat posed by the lack of synthesis between capitalism and communism is environmental degradation. Capitalism's focus on growth and profit maximization has often led to the exploitation of natural resources and environmental neglect. The concept of externalities, where the social and environmental costs of economic activities are not reflected in market prices, has resulted in pollution, deforestation, and climate change (Ostrom, 1990).

While communism, in theory, advocates for collective ownership and stewardship of resources, historical examples such as the environmental disasters in the Soviet Union reveal that centralized planning does not necessarily result in sustainable practices (Feshbach & Friendly, 1992).

A synthesis of capitalist innovation and communist environmental stewardship is essential to address the global environmental crisis. Without it, the world risks reaching irreversible tipping points, where the damage to ecosystems becomes irreparable. This would have catastrophic consequences, including the displacement of millions of people due to rising sea levels, increased frequency of extreme weather events, and the loss of biodiversity, which is crucial for maintaining ecological balance and human survival (Rockström et al., 2009).

Social Disintegration and Alienation

Finally, the failure to synthesize capitalist and communist ideals could lead to social disintegration and alienation. Capitalism's emphasis on individualism and competition can erode social bonds and community ties, leading to a sense of alienation and isolation among individuals. Durkheim's concept of anomie, where individuals feel disconnected from the collective conscience of society, is particularly relevant in this context (Durkheim, 1897). The relentless pursuit of material success in capitalist societies often comes at the expense of social and familial relationships, contributing to a decline in mental health and well-being.

On the other hand, communism's focus on collective identity and social solidarity can lead to the suppression of individual autonomy and creativity, as seen in the enforced conformity of communist regimes. A synthesis of these ideologies could provide a balance between individual fulfillment and collective well-being, fostering a sense of belonging and purpose in society.

If society fails to achieve this synthesis, the result could be a fragmented and polarized world, where individuals retreat into isolated, self-interested communities, and the social fabric becomes increasingly frayed. This could manifest in rising mental health issues, declining civic engagement, and the proliferation of extremist ideologies that exploit feelings of alienation and resentment.

The synthesis of capitalist and communist ideals is not merely a theoretical exercise but a practical necessity for the future of society. The failure to reconcile the efficiency and innovation of capitalism with the equity and social justice goals of communism poses significant risks, including deepening economic inequality, political instability, environmental degradation, and social disintegration. As we confront the challenges of the 21st century, it is imperative that we move beyond the ideological dichotomy that has defined the past century and work towards a more integrated and holistic approach to economic and social organization. Only by synthesizing the strengths of both capitalism and communism can we hope to build a more just, sustainable, and harmonious society for future generations.

References


- Arendt, H. (1951). The Origins of Totalitarianism. Schocken Books.
- Bakunin, M. (1873). Statism and Anarchy. Cambridge University Press.
- Castells, M. (2010). The Rise of the Network Society. Wiley-Blackwell.
- Dahl, R. A. (1989). Democracy and Its Critics. Yale University Press.
- Djilas, M. (1957). The New Class: An Analysis of the Communist System. Harcourt, Brace.
- Durkheim, E. (1897). Suicide: A Study in Sociology. Free Press.
- Feshbach, M., & Friendly, A. (1992). Ecocide in the USSR: Health and Nature Under Siege. Basic Books.
- Freud, S. (1930). Civilization and Its Discontents. W. W. Norton & Company.
- Harvey, D. (2005). A Brief History of Neoliberalism. Oxford University Press.
- Held, D., & McGrew, A. (2002). Globalization/Anti-Globalization: Beyond the Great Divide. Polity Press.
- Kant, I. (1795). Perpetual Peace: A Philosophical Sketch. Hackett Publishing Company.
- Kropotkin, P. (1902). Mutual Aid: A Factor of Evolution. McClure, Philips & Co.
- Levitas, R. (2013). Utopia as Method: The Imaginary Reconstitution of Society. Palgrave Macmillan.

- Levitsky, S., & Ziblatt, D. (2018). How Democracies Die. Crown.
- Marx, K. (1867). Das Kapital. Verlag von Otto Meisner.
- Meadows, D. H., Meadows, D. L., Randers, J., & Behrens III, W. W. (1972). The Limits to Growth: A Report for the Club of Rome's Project on the Predicament of Mankind. Universe Books.
- Mill, J. S. (1859). On Liberty. J.W. Parker and Son.
- More, T. (1516). Utopia. Yale University Press.
- Ostrom, E. (1990). Governing the Commons: The Evolution of Institutions for Collective Action. Cambridge University Press.
- Piketty, T. (2014). Capital in the Twenty-First Century. Belknap Press.
- Popper, K. (1945). The Open Society and Its Enemies. Routledge.
- Rawls, J. (1971). A Theory of Justice. Harvard University Press.
- Rockström, J., Steffen, W., Noone, K., et al. (2009). A safe operating space for humanity. Nature, 461(7263), 472-475.
- Sen, A. (1999). Development as Freedom. Oxford University Press.
- Stiglitz, J. E. (2002). Globalization and Its Discontents. W. W. Norton & Company.
- Stiglitz, J. E. (2012). The Price of Inequality: How Today's Divided Society Endangers Our Future. W.W. Norton & Company.
- Zuboff, S. (2019). The Age of Surveillance Capitalism: The Fight for a Human Future at the New Frontier of Power. PublicAffairs.

## Conclusion

### Summary of Key Insights

This book has explored the complex dynamics between capitalism, socialism, and communism, tracing their historical developments, theoretical foundations, and practical implementations. We have delved into the complexities of synthesizing these ideologies, proposing a contribution-based economic model that seeks to harmonize individual incentives with collective welfare. Through a critical analysis of historical case studies, technological advancements, and governance structures, we have identified both the challenges and opportunities in creating a more equitable economic system.

Capitalism's strengths lie in its ability to foster innovation and economic growth, driven by market competition and private ownership (Smith, 1776). Weaknesses include the tendency toward income inequality and environmental degradation (Piketty, 2014). Communism, with its emphasis on equality and collective ownership, offers a vision of a classless society but has historically struggled with authoritarianism and economic inefficiencies (Marx, 1867; Harvey, 2010). By integrating elements from both systems, we can develop a new economic model that balances and aligns the strengths of each while addressing their respective shortcomings.

Throughout this book, we have highlighted the importance of technology, particularly blockchain and AI, in creating transparent and fair economic systems. These technologies can ensure that contributions are accurately measured and rewarded, aligning economic incentives with the common good (Tapscott & Tapscott, 2016). Furthermore, we have emphasized the role of governance and regulation in overcoming human interference, mitigating corruption, and promoting ethical practices in economics (Stiglitz, 2012).

## The Future of Economic Systems

As we look to the future, the evolution of economic systems will likely be shaped by several key trends: the increasing integration of technology into economic processes, the growing importance of sustainability, and the need for global cooperation. The convergence of capitalism and communism into a synthesized economic model could offer a viable path forward, combining the dynamism of markets with the equity goals of social planning.

Technological advancements, particularly in the fields of AI and blockchain, will play a crucial role in shaping the future economy. These technologies have the potential to create more efficient and transparent systems, reduce transaction costs, and empower individuals and communities. Nevertheless, they also pose challenges, such as the risk of exacerbating inequality and the need for powerful and effective regulatory frameworks to ensure ethical use (Brynjolfsson & McAfee, 2014; Zuboff, 2019).

Sustainability will become an increasingly important consideration as the global community grapples with the impacts of climate change and resource depletion. Economic systems of the future must prioritize environmental stewardship and sustainable development, integrating these goals into the core of economic policy and practice (Meadows et al., 1972).

Global cooperation will be essential in addressing the complex, interconnected challenges of the 21st century. From climate change to economic inequality, the issues we face transcend national borders and require collective action. Strengthening international institutions and fostering a sense of global solidarity will be crucial in building a more just and sustainable world (Held & McGrew, 2002).

## Call to Action: Building a Fair and Equitable Society

The insights gained from this exploration of economic systems are not merely theoretical; they serve as a call to action for policymakers, business leaders, and citizens alike. Building a fair and equitable society requires collective effort, guided by principles of justice, sustainability, and inclusivity.

1. Policy Reform: Governments must take proactive steps to reform economic policies, ensuring that they promote both economic growth and social equity. This includes implementing progressive taxation, investing in universal basic services, and regulating markets to prevent exploitation and environmental harm.
2. Corporate Responsibility: Businesses have a critical role to play in building a fair economy. By embracing corporate social responsibility, adopting sustainable practices, and considering the interests of all stakeholders, companies can contribute to a more just and equitable society (Porter & Kramer, 2011).
3. Citizen Engagement: Citizens must remain engaged in the political process, advocating for policies that promote social justice and environmental sustainability. Participatory governance and grassroots movements are essential in holding leaders accountable and driving positive change.
4. Education and Innovation: Education systems should focus on cultivating ethical leadership and innovation, equipping future generations with the skills and values needed to navigate the complexities of the modern world. Innovation should be directed toward solving social and environmental challenges, rather than merely maximizing profit.

## Final Reflection

Is utopia achievable? While a perfect society may always remain just out of reach, the pursuit of utopia is a worthwhile endeavor. It challenges us to continuously strive for a better world, to question the status quo, and to envision new possibilities. By synthesizing the best elements of capitalism, communism, and emerging economic models, we can build a more just, equitable, and sustainable society. The journey toward utopia is not about reaching perfection but about making incremental progress away from an imperfect world. Together, we can take the steps necessary to create an economy that serves the common good and fosters the well-being of all people.

References

- Brynjolfsson, E., & McAfee, A. (2014). The Second Machine Age: Work, Progress, and Prosperity in a Time of Brilliant Technologies. W. W. Norton & Company.
- Harvey, D. (2010). The Enigma of Capital: And the Crises of Capitalism. Oxford University Press.
- Held, D., & McGrew, A. (2002). Globalization/Anti-Globalization: Beyond the Great Divide. Polity Press.
- Marx, K. (1867). Das Kapital. Verlag von Otto Meisner.
- Meadows, D. H., Meadows, D. L., Randers, J., & Behrens III, W. W. (1972). The Limits to Growth: A Report for the Club of Rome's Project on the Predicament of Mankind. Universe Books.
- Piketty, T. (2014). Capital in the Twenty-First Century. Harvard University Press.
- Porter, M. E., & Kramer, M. R. (2011). Creating shared value: How to reinvent capitalism

—and unleash a wave of innovation and growth. Harvard Business Review, 89(1/2), 62-77.

- Smith, A. (1776). An Inquiry into the Nature and Causes of the Wealth of Nations. W. Strahan and T. Cadell.
- Stiglitz, J. E. (2012). The Price of Inequality: How Today's Divided Society Endangers Our

Future. W. W. Norton & Company.

- Tapscott, D., & Tapscott, A. (2016). Blockchain Revolution: How the Technology Behind Bitcoin Is Changing Money, Business, and the World. Penguin.
- Zuboff, S. (2019). The Age of Surveillance Capitalism: The Fight for a Human Future at the New Frontier of Power. PublicAffairs.

## Appendices

Appendix A: Glossary of Terms

1. Capitalism: An economic system characterized by private ownership of the means of production, where goods and services are produced for profit in a competitive market.
2. Communism: A political and economic ideology advocating for a classless society in which the means of production are owned collectively, and wealth is distributed according to need.
3. Blockchain: A decentralized digital ledger technology that records transactions across many computers in such a way that the registered transactions cannot be altered retroactively.
4. Contribution-Based Economy: An economic model where resources and rewards are distributed based on the value that individuals and organizations contribute to society, rather than on market competition or state control.
5. Corporate Social Responsibility (CSR): A business model that helps a company be socially accountable to itself, its stakeholders, and the public, by promoting sustainability, ethical practices, and community engagement.
6. Decentralization: The distribution of administrative powers or functions of a central authority over a less concentrated area or among multiple entities.
7. Neoclassical Economics: A mainstream economic school of thought that emphasizes the determination of goods, outputs, and income distributions through supply and demand within markets.
8. Utopia: An imagined society that possesses highly desirable or nearly perfect qualities for its citizens, often used to describe an ideal community or society.
9. Sustainable Development: Economic development that is conducted without depletion of natural resources, ensuring that environmental, social, and economic needs are met for future generations.
10. Progressive Taxation: A tax system in which the rate of taxation increases as the taxable amount increases, often

used to reduce inequality by placing a higher tax burden on wealthier individuals.

Appendix B: Detailed Case Studies

1. The Soviet Experiment
    - Overview: The Soviet Union's attempt to establish a communist society, focusing on its successes in industrialization and failures in maintaining economic efficiency and individual freedoms.
    - Key Insights: Analysis of the Five-Year Plans, collectivization, and the eventual collapse of the Soviet system.
    - References: Nove, A. (1983). The Economics of Feasible Socialism. Allen & Unwin.
2. Scandinavian Socialism
    - Overview: An examination of the Nordic model of socialism in countries like Sweden, Norway, and Denmark, which successfully blends capitalist dynamism with comprehensive welfare systems.
    - Key Insights: The role of public welfare, progressive taxation, and economic competitiveness in creating a sustainable social system.
    - References: Andersen, T. M., et al. (2007). The Nordic Model: Embracing Globalization and Sharing Risks. The Research Institute of the Finnish Economy.
3. Fair Trade Movement
    - Overview: A case study on the Fair Trade movement, which seeks to ensure that producers in developing countries are paid fairly and that their goods are produced under ethical conditions.
    - Key Insights: The impact of Fair Trade on global supply chains, sustainability, and economic justice.
    - References: Raynolds, L. T., et al. (2007). Fair Trade: The Challenges of Transforming Globalization. Routledge.
4. Open-Source Software Development
    - Overview: Exploration of the open-source software movement as a practical example of a contribution-based model in the digital economy.

- Key Insights: The role of community collaboration, reputation systems, and the creation of public goods.
- References: Weber, S. (2004). The Success of Open Source. Harvard University Press.

Appendix C: Methodology for Measuring Contributions

1. Social Impact Metrics
   - Definition: Tools and frameworks used to measure the social, environmental, and economic impact of activities, such as the Social Return on Investment (SROI) framework.
   - Application: Examples of how SROI and similar metrics can be used to assess the value of contributions in a contribution-based economic system.
   - References: Nicholls, J., et al. (2009). A Guide to Social Return on Investment. The SROI Network.
2. Collaborative Rating Systems
   - Definition: Systems in which peer reviews and community ratings are used to evaluate the contributions of individuals and organizations.
   - Application: Examples from online platforms and how these systems can be adapted for broader economic use.
   - References: Benkler, Y. (2017). Peer production, the commons, and the future of the firm. Strategic Organization, 15(2), 264-274.
3. Data-Driven Analytics
   - Definition: The use of big data and AI to track and analyze contributions in real- time, providing a dynamic and ongoing assessment of value creation.
   - Application: Case studies of how data analytics are used in modern businesses and their potential application in contribution-based economies.
   - References: Brynjolfsson, E., & McAfee, A. (2014). The Second Machine Age: Work, Progress, and Prosperity in a Time of Brilliant Technologies. W. W. Norton & Company.

Appendix D: Additional Resources and Readings

1. Books
   - The Wealth of Networks: How Social Production Transforms Markets and Freedom by Yochai Benkler
   - Capital in the Twenty-First Century by Thomas Piketty
   - Blockchain Revolution: How the Technology Behind Bitcoin Is Changing Money,

Business, and the World by Don Tapscott and Alex Tapscott
   - On Liberty and Freedom- by Jeremy Dean Harrison (2024)
   - Performance Efficacy- The Future of Mankind's Motivation and How We Can Contribute Value to Make It Better- by Jeremy Dean Harrison (2024)
   - Performance Efficacy for Artists and Athletes- by Jeremy Dean Harrison (2024)
   - The Contribution Revolution- by Jeremy Dean Harrison (2024)
2. Journals
   - The American Economic Review
   - Journal of Economic Perspectives
   - World Development
3. Reports
   - The Limits to Growth by The Club of Rome
   - The Stern Review: The Economics of Climate Change by Nicholas Stern
   - Globalization and Its Discontents by Joseph E. Stiglitz
   - Understanding Good and Evil and how to Overcome Challenges through the Philosophies of Kant- by Jeremy Dean Harrison (2024).
4. Websites
   - The World Bank: www.worldbank.org
   - United Nations Sustainable Development Goals: www.un.org/sustainabledevelopment
   - Transparency International: www.transparency.org

I forgot what I said.
Let me go back and read it again.

Made in the USA
Monee, IL
04 November 2026

67383111R00066